People
Management

People Management

Rosemary Thomson

ORION
BUSINESS
BOOKS

First published in Great Britain in 1998 by
Orion Business
An imprint of The Orion Publishing Group Ltd
Orion House, 5 Upper St Martin's Lane, London WC2H 9EA

A CIP catalogue record for this book
is available from the British Library

ISBN 0–75281–359–5

Typeset by Deltatype Ltd, Birkenhead, Merseyside
Printed in Great Britain by
Clays Ltd, St Ives plc

Contents

Introduction

'Management problems always turn out to be people problems.'

(J. Peet, 1988)

➡ WHY DO PEOPLE NEED TO BE MANAGED?

I have begun every chapter in this book with a quotation that I would like you to think about before you read on. Do you agree or disagree with the writer's view?

You might think, in this case, that the author is being rather cynical. After all, you could argue that money – or its lack – can cause considerable problems in business. You can also have problems with faulty machinery, equipment or vehicles, substandard supplies, late deliveries and so on. But if you think about what lies behind the problems, it is quite often the case that human error or decisions are the root cause. The management of money is a human task. The machinery or equipment may have been assembled incorrectly in the factory, or the operator may have failed to ensure that it is regularly serviced or cleaned; one of your drivers may be at fault if a vehicle is off the road; someone may have made a decision to offer you supplies below standard, and it may well be a human reason that deliveries are not being made on time.

One of the main reasons why people need to be managed is to prevent them being, or creating, problems for you as their manager and for the organisation as a whole. Another reason is that people are a very expensive resource. In many organisations today, despite downsizing and the rise of technology, the annual wage bill exceeds any other single item on the balance sheet. As you will see in Chapter 9, making the wrong decisions about who to employ can lead to very costly mistakes.

People are very valuable to the organisation because each individual brings with them a wealth of knowledge and experience. This knowledge and experience is increased through working in the organisation and can be thought of as human capital. This doesn't show up on the balance sheet, but perhaps it should be there as an asset to offset the costs of employment.

People can also be problems, however. We all know about the ones that are. They are the people who don't perform well, who cause trouble either overtly or through spreading rumours and alarm, who go off sick as often as they can get away with it, who come in late or leave early. They are the ones who constantly complain or argue or who cannot seem to find a good word for anyone else. Part of this can be laid at the door of individual differences in human nature, part may be due to their own problems outside work. And much may be due to the way they are managed, or mismanaged, in the work situation.

During the early nineties, the worldwide recession changed the nature of 'jobs for life': they ceased to exist. From then on, organisations have 'slimmed down', restructured, downsized and disappeared. People have lost the jobs that they had expected to be secure for the rest of their working lives, and many have not got other jobs. Many of those who have remained in work have worried that they would be the next to go. There has been an increase in part-time work and in short-term contracts, neither of which offers any measure of job security. Employee stress has become an occupational disease. Some degree of stress at work is inevitable, but excessive stress, according to Peter Warr (1992), '... impairs work effectiveness, reduces productivity, and costs the organisation money.' Not only can an organisation lose an employee's time if he or she is off work from a stress-related illness, but it may also have to pay for health care and compensation claims.

There have been other changes in working practices in the last decade. The use of technology has certainly increased, changing the ways in which jobs are performed. Some people find it hard to cope with change, particularly if they feel they have not been consulted about it or involved in decisions that affect them and their jobs. And there is increasing evidence that the attitude of employers and managers to employees has changed from one that was essentially concerned with consultation and participation to a much more pragmatic approach, probably as a result of a world recession, downsizing and the increasing practice of contracting out all but core business.

➡ HOW CAN THIS BOOK HELP YOU?

You have probably had a quick look at the chapter headings in this book and, presumably, found some of them to be areas of management in which you are interested or which you need to find out about. Each chapter is self-standing and covers a particular topic related to managing people.

Chapter 1 is concerned with you as a manager of people, your roles and responsibilities and your preferred leadership style. There will be checklists to help you analyse the way in which you lead others, what sources of power you have, how you can make enough time to manage your staff effectively and how to recognise stress at work and do something about it. You will also be looking at how you manage *with* other people – your colleagues and your own line manager.

Managers need to talk to their staff and other people with whom they work. Communication is the topic covered in Chapter 2. Talking face-to-face may not, however, always be feasible or the best way of communicating in certain circumstances, and we look at the use of written and electronic communication as well as the best way to make meetings productive.

Chapter 3 is called 'Making decisions and plans'. As a manager, you are likely to have this as a major part of your job and, often, the planning and decision making you do concerns other people. Some decisions are easy to make but some are more difficult, and we look at ways in which planning and decision making in general can be made more rational.

Motivation and rewards are the topic areas in Chapter 4. Once you have recruited staff you want to keep them (remember the investment aspect). You also want to keep your existing 'human capital', but that means gaining commitment from the people you work with and rewarding them appropriately. This may include financial rewards, but other types of incentives can be equally important – sometimes even more important – than money.

Managers should be involved in monitoring performance. Using an appraisal system, however informal, is one way of doing this, as discussed in Chapter 5. But there are a number of ways in which appraisals can involve other people (such as work colleagues and subordinates) to give a more rounded picture. Once-a-year appraisal may be the kind of system that operates in your organisation, but that is usually too infrequent to have any impact on daily performance. One answer to this problem is to have ongoing performance reviews to ensure that objectives are being met. If they aren't, you and the members of your staff have the opportunity to take some action to improve matters.

Since more responsibility for training and development is nowadays passed to line managers to organise (if not carry out), the subject matter of Chapters 6 and 7 should help you analyse ways in which you can provide these opportunities for your staff. There are a number of options, both formal and informal, in-house and external, and these are covered in Chapter 6. In Chapter 7 we look at some methods of training and development in more depth – induction, coaching, mentoring and delegation. These are methods that any manager can use without much cost to the organisation – apart from the very real cost in some cases in terms of a manager's time.

In Chapter 8, we look at teams and how they can be managed effectively. More and more organisations are working in project teams, using groups of 'experts' to form and re-form depending on the particular task. Here, the manager may not necessarily always be the leader; this role may be handed over to the acknowledged expert, or leadership of the team may alter depending on different phases of the task.

At some point, you are likely to be involved in bringing in new staff, and recruitment and selection are the topics covered in Chapter 9. As I said earlier, selection decisions can be very expensive and it is important to make the selection process as reliable as possible.

Finally, in Chapter 10, we look at difficult interviews – the kinds of situations many managers would prefer not to happen. But these kinds of incidents – harassment, violence, grievance, disciplinary actions etc – *do* happen in business life and far too often the average manager is completely unprepared for them. Again, looking at these incidents in financial terms, if they are mishandled they can cost the organisation a considerable amount in compensation. The manager's aim must be to prevent such conflictual incidents from escalating to the point where the individual feels so aggrieved that he or she decides to take industrial or other action, and Chapter 10 gives some guidelines.

➡ INTRODUCING CHRIS

At the end of each chapter, you will meet Chris. Chris is a fictional manager who encounters real-life situations. Chris could be male or female, work in any organisation of any size in any of the public, private, service or non-profit sectors. In fact, Chris could be you. Based on your reading of the chapter and your own experience, we ask you to offer Chris some advice on how to cope with the tricky situations that crop up in any manager's daily life – or could crop up in your role as a manager.

References

Peet J., 'Management Consultancy', *The Economist*, 13 February 1988.

Warr P., 'Job features and excessive stress' in R. Jenkins and N. Coney (eds), *Prevention of Mental Ill-health at Work* (HMSO, Norwich, 1992).

Chapter 1
Your role in people management

'Managers may be born but they also have to be made.'

(Sir David Steel, 1982)

Do you agree with Sir David Steel's view of managers? Are 'managerial ability' or 'leadership' characteristics that you can inherit and that are with you from birth? Or do they need to be developed through experience and training?

➡ MANAGERS AND LEADERSHIP STYLE

Early researchers into management believed that leadership qualities were innate, and they studied acknowledged leaders to see if they could find a set of common characteristics. They were never able to agree completely on this set of characteristics, although, generally speaking, most studies did include intelligence, initiative, self-assurance and the ability to take an overall view of events as common traits in most leaders. Think about a manager you admire: does he or she possess these leadership qualities? And what about a manager you do not admire: are any of these qualities missing?

Nevertheless, most people dismiss the idea of 'born leaders' since so many other factors are likely to come into play. Upbringing and education, for example, will have some effect, but remember that the illiterate leader of a street gang can be as powerful a figure to the people who are in that gang as the highly educated president of a country can be to its citizens. As you will see later on in Chapter 8, even though the manager may normally be the leader, this is not always the case. In a project team, for example, it may be someone who is expert in a particular field vital to the success of the project who takes over the leadership role.

There used to be a debate about whether all managers were leaders or whether all managers *needed* to be leaders. These days, that debate has largely disappeared. More and more organisations are devolving the responsibility for managing staff to their line managers. Even in large organisations, Personnel or Human Resource Departments are more involved in the regulation of staff systems and record keeping and in providing training and development opportunities than in areas such as appraisal or career management. It is now accepted that it is good practice to involve line managers in decisions about selecting new staff or promoting staff for whom they are responsible. And in cases of grievance or trouble making, it is an individual's manager who is usually the first person to be approached. In this way, nearly all managers have some responsibility for leadership within their area of responsibility.

There are, however, different ways of leading and Checklist 1.1 below gives some examples of statements made by people who consider they are leaders in the management sense. Go through these statements and see which one(s) seem to you to represent an ideal leadership style.

Checklist 1.1   Which style of leadership?

(1) I was appointed as a manager in this company and that gives me the authority and status to make decisions and tell my staff to carry them out. After all, they are subordinate to me; if they made decisions, they would all be managers. They need to know who is boss and to respect me as their manager, otherwise nothing would get done around here.

(2) I have responsibility as a manager to decide what needs to be done and how it should be done. But it's no good just telling the people who work for me that they have to get on with the job. I need to explain to them why and how it needs to be done within a certain timescale, so that they understand why I want it done that way.

(3) I am paid to make the decisions round here – it's part of

my job. But I'm very conscious that my staff have a tremendous amount of experience and expertise that I would be a fool not to use. So when I have an idea about something, I call a meeting of those involved and invite them to ask questions about the idea so that we can clarify how it can be put into practice.

(4) Like the manager in (3) above, I respect the expertise of my staff. They are the ones carrying out the work and know best how it can be done effectively. So I call them together when I have to make a decision about how a task is to be tackled and tell them how I think it might be undertaken. They have their say, though, and quite often my original ideas will be changed and theirs will be used as well.

(5) I don't believe in solving problems on my own, and so when one occurs I ask my staff to think about it and make suggestions as to how we might solve it. Then I make a decision based on those suggestions.

(6) When we have a problem or are asked to take on something new, we meet as a team where I am a team member in the same way as everyone else. I explain what we have to do and then the team decides how we should carry it out. That way it is everyone's decision and all my staff feel they have a stake in it.

(7) I believe in giving my staff as much freedom as possible. Of course, there have to be limits, and I decide what those are. I explain what has to be done and why, and sometimes how it should be done. After that, I leave it to them and I don't interfere.

It would not be surprising if you agreed with more than one of the statements in Checklist 1.1 – or if you agreed with none of them since they are stereotypes. The statements are based on a model of leadership style through decision making devised by the American researchers Tannenbaum and Schmidt (1958). As you probably realised, the statements ranged from a very autocratic leadership style (1) to a very permissive one (7), and most managers would probably consider they led using one or more of the styles between (2) and (6).

However, is one style of leadership suitable for all occasions, all organisations, and all people? How would a very autocratic manager fare in an organisation where people were used to taking considerable responsibility for decisions about how they worked? And do all people actually want to take that kind of responsibility? If they don't – and I would argue that there are quite a lot of people who prefer someone else to tell them what to do – what would their reaction be to a manager who left them to get on with things and expected them to make decisions on their own?

Modern theory argues that leadership needs to be dependent on four factors:

- the leader and his or her preferred management style
- the job and how it needs to be carried out
- the people and how they feel as individuals about taking responsibility
- the organisation in which the job is being carried out and the accepted way things are done there

However, this may mean that managers need to change the way in which they lead and manage their staff if their preferred style conflicts with the job that needs to be done, the people carrying it out or the way the organisation expects it to be undertaken. For example, when a job needs to be done within a very tight timescale and everyone knows what has to be done, there really isn't time or need for excessive consultation and meetings. So, a manager who prefers to work like the one in (7) on Checklist 1.1. would be better advised in this case to make any decisions necessary, tell the staff about them, and ensure they were clear about getting the job done; that manager would need to move to a style like the one in (3) or (4) on the checklist. On the other hand, if the task was a new one and very complex, and the staff were inexperienced, the manager should probably act like the manager in (5), (6) or (7).

Finally on the topic of leadership, Checklist 1.2 from *The Personnel Manager's Factbook* (Gee, 1997) suggests ways in which a manager can be an effective leader. You might like to assess yourself against the suggestions below.

Checklist 1.2 **The effective leader**

- looks at the task and decides what his or her role is
- acquires knowledge needed to carry out the task effectively
- adequately briefs others both in the detail of what is required and what the limits of their authority are
- considers the problems of others, i.e. 'starts where the other person is'
- delegates decisions and responsibility where possible
- is fair and consistent
- is prepared to accept criticism
- helps others without doing their work for them
- acts as a resource person
- makes decisions (rather than prevaricates)
- understands how leadership operates in a group situation
- is aware of individuals within a group

➡ THE MANAGER'S POWER BASE

Two important factors that influence how effective a manager is as a leader are the type and amount of power that that person holds. Someone with very little power or authority will have a hard time gaining respect if he or she behaves as an autocratic leader. Notice I said 'power *or* authority' for they are not the same thing.

Power is the ability of a person to influence other people. There are a number of different kinds of power in organisations, as you will see in Checklist 1.3. Authority is the right to exercise power – it legitimises the use of power. You can be given power through having responsibility for resources that other people need or want – money, materials, expertise and so on – or through your relationship to other people. For example, blackmailers have power over their victims but no authority; they have no *right* to be blackmailers.

Checklist 1.3 outlines the different kinds of power that generally exist in organisations, which are discussed in more detail below.

Go through the list and decide which sources of power you have as a manager. You might also like to think about other people in your organisation and the kind of power they can exert.

| Checklist 1.3 | Sources of power in organisations |

- position
- resource
- expert
- social
- personal
- information
- referent
- reward
- coercive
- negative

Position power

This is power that is very similar to authority since it is based on a person's role or position in an organisation. Most managers will have this type of power in varying degrees. A junior manager, for example, does not have as much position power as the chief executive. Position power means you have the authority to do certain things, such as allocate and organise the work of your staff, set budgets and authorise expenditure, draw up holiday rotas and so on. But this authority will have limits – again, you are not likely to have the same authority as the head of your organisation.

Resource power

Resource power is control over the money, people, supplies and machinery (amongst other resources) that organisations and the people in them need to carry out their work. Most people will only have resource power based on a single resource, but if that resource is scarce and is one that everyone needs, that person's power level can be very high. For example, if your department wants to invest in new technology and you do not have the authority to ensure this can be paid for, whoever holds the budget for that kind of expenditure has considerable resource power over you.

Expert power

You may have a particular talent or expertise that, to be a source of power, needs to be accepted and recognised by those over whom it is exercised. It usually needs to be useful to the organisation as well. You may well play a great game of tennis, which involves considerable expertise, but that kind of talent doesn't generally increase the productivity of the organisation! The most common sources of expert power in organisations are technical knowledge (knowledge about the product or service the organisation delivers) and process knowledge (knowledge about how to get things done).

Social power

This kind of power is based on who you know and how effective you are at getting things done because you know certain people. This means being involved in an organisational network of other managers and experts, often including people from outside the organisation, such as clients, customers, suppliers and colleagues in other organisations. Unfortunately, this kind of power can be subject to abuse, such as when it is used to further an individual's own career or make their life easier.

Personal power

This is the kind of factor the early researchers into leadership style were seeking when they were trying to define 'charisma'. It is based on a person's personality and behaviour, their intelligence, confidence, charm, drive, friendliness and so on. If people respect you for the kind of person you are and the way you behave towards them, then you can be said to have personal power.

Information power

If you, and only you, have access to particular information, this can be a source of power. You can decide who is to get what information and how much, what information is relevant, what information is best kept on a confidential basis. The more people need the information you have, the higher is your power level. Information power can be a mixture of resource power and expert power.

Referent power

This is the kind of vicarious power that results from having been asked to undertake a task by, for example, a senior manager or director. Some of that person's power is transferred across and increases the power of the subordinate, who can ask for things to be done '... because the Chief Executive wants it.'

Reward power

As a manager, you have the power to bestow or withhold rewards such as promotion, merit increases, bonuses etc. This is reward power.

Coercive power

Coercion these days is usually subtle. Hints can be dropped about sanctions that might operate if something is not done or a specific task not undertaken.

Negative power

This is the kind of power that stops things being done. It can be used to create delays, prevent action or distort information. You need to be very careful if you want to exercise negative power, ensuring that its outcome will be in the best interests of other people and the organisation. For example, blocking ideas for change can have two outcomes: it can prevent a necessary change from taking place, one that is going to benefit individuals and the organisation; or it can slow down the pace of change, giving time for wider consultation, rethinking and, in the end, a better quality of action.

John Hunt (1986) advocates the sensitive use of power by managers and suggests the following guidelines:

- be honest and open with others
- avoid unnecessary power struggles
- don't be afraid of power – people with power *do* make better managers
- negotiation is essential in all processes
- share your power with others – empower others by involving them in decisions
- recognise the legitimate power of others such as experts

➡ THE MANAGER'S ROLE

Managers often complain that they are too busy fire fighting and managing crises to know (let alone do) what they really should be doing. This can also be a result of poor time management, which we shall be looking at in the next section. So, what *should* you be doing?

One classification of what managers do was provided by Henri Fayol, a French mining engineer and later Managing Director of a large French mining and metallurgical enterprise. Fayol suggested (1949) that most managers, no matter at what level or in what kind of organisation they work, carry out the following activities:

- forecasting and planning – looking ahead
- organising – workloads, schedules, how things are done
- commanding – leadership, setting an example to their staff, motivating their staff
- co-ordinating – ensuring what is being done is consistent with what is needed and with the other work being carried out in the organisation
- controlling – checking that work is being carried out satisfactorily

and, if necessary, making adjustments to the way it is carried
out

Look at Fayol's list of activities: is that what you do as a
manager? Are there other activities not covered by Fayol under
those headings that you carry out as a manager? Do you find that
you are carrying out more activities under one or more of Fayol's
headings than under others? Is this an effective and efficient way
of managing? Take a few minutes to think about these questions.

In the mid-1990s, the Institute of Management in the UK
commissioned a number of surveys into the ways in which
managers work, what they do and what they should be doing.
Look at Checklist 1.4, which lists the areas identified by the
authors of one of the reports, *Management Development to the
Millennium* (BIM, 1994), where managers need to develop the
ability to cope with management in the twenty-first century.
Which of these abilities do you currently have and exercise in your
present job, and which might you need to develop?

Checklist 1.4   Managerial abilities for the twenty-first century

Managers in the twenty-first century will need to:

- respond to and manage change
- manage cross-functional teams
- take the initiative
- adhere to corporate or organisational goals
- understand the operations of the whole organisation
- empower staff and others to develop their skills
- manage their own development as a manager
- maintain motivation in their staff
- maintain their own motivation

Checklist 1.5, based on the same report, lists in priority order the
skills it is judged that managers will need to manage successfully in
the future. Again, go down the list and assess which of these skills
you already possess and use in your job and which you would need
to develop.

Checklist 1.5 **Managerial skills for the twenty-first century**

- strategic thinking
- responding to and managing change
- an orientation towards 'total quality' and customer satisfaction
- financial management
- encouraging and facilitating the contribution of others
- understanding the role of information and information technology
- verbal communication
- knowledge and understanding of the organisation
- risk assessment in decision making

Few managers will possess all of the abilities and skills in Checklists 1.4 and 1.5, and you will be given some ideas of ways in which you can develop yourself as a manager in Chapter 6 of this book. What the lists do is give you an indication of how you may need to change and develop in your working practice as a manager – a sense of your own future development needs.

➡ MANAGING TIME

I pointed out at the beginning of the last section that many managers may be too busy because they fail to manage their time effectively. Not only that, but they may fail to manage the time of the people for whom they are responsible, creating an inefficient working group. As a manager, your time is a valuable resource and, in particular, you need to find (i.e. *make*) time to manage the people for whom you are responsible. Too often, we hear people complain about their managers in terms such as these:

- 'He never seems to have a free moment just to talk to me.'
- 'If I go in to ask her something, she is always too busy to listen and tells me to come back later.'
- 'I made an appointment to see my manager, and he kept on interrupting the conversation to answer the phone.'

- 'She says things like "Everything all right then?" and never stops to hear the answer.'

Do you recognise yourself as the manager is any of those statements? Or do you recognise any of your colleagues or senior managers?

Think about the last time you had an important piece of work to do, but you failed to complete it on schedule through lack of time. Which of the factors in Checklist 1.6 might have been the reason for this failure?

Checklist 1.6   Time wasters

- Getting in to work late because of traffic congestion, late train, missing the bus etc.
- Starting an item of work late because you had other things to do first.
- Starting an item of work late because something unexpected and urgent needed to be done first.
- Interruptions from telephone calls.
- Interruptions from people wanting to see you.
- Lack of essential information that you needed to complete the work.
- The word processor or some other essential piece of equipment breaking down.
- A work crisis that had to be dealt with immediately.

The work just took much longer than you had anticipated.

Of course, there might have been other reasons why the work was never completed, but let's look at each of these time wasters in turn and see how some of them might have been avoided.

Getting into work late

You are not in control of public transport nor of road conditions, but if this is a fairly common occurrence, you are definitely going to have to leave home earlier or find an alternative method of getting into work. Many managers prefer to come into work earlier than is required so that they get some undisturbed time at the start of the working day to organise what they and their staff are going to do.

Doing other things first

If the work you had to do was so important, nothing should take priority over it apart from a real emergency. Trying to get other tasks out of the way is often just an excuse for not getting down to the real work that needs to be done. It is highly likely that all of the tasks you undertook, and that made you late in starting the important piece of work, could have waited until later or been delegated to someone else.

Interruptions from phone calls

If you have a secretary, ask him or her to filter your calls in order to ensure you are not disturbed unless the call is really important. Few calls cannot be deflected through taking a message and promising that you will call back. Alternatively, make an arrangement with a colleague to take your calls in return for doing the same for them when they are particularly busy. As a last resort, take your telephone off-line.

Interruptions from people

Operate a 'closed door' policy when you need uninterrupted time. Ensure your staff understand that they are welcome in your office to talk to you or ask questions when the door is open but not when it is closed. You may need to make sure that there is someone else who can help them when you are in your closed-door mode – this person may be a colleague or someone else to whom you have temporarily delegated some of your authority.

Lack of essential information

This is really lack of planning. If you know in advance that you have a certain task to perform and a certain time within which to perform it, you should make sure you have all the necessary resources, including information, to hand by making an early assessment of all that is required to do the job.

Breakdown of equipment

You cannot always anticipate this kind of problem but having a backup is useful. If you depend on a personal computer or word processor, for example, ensure you have access to another machine if yours breaks down. Make sure any equipment or machinery you are going to need is in good working order before you start – not immediately before you start but sufficiently beforehand.

A work crisis

These happen and, in the nature of crises, they are unexpected and unanticipated. However, if you are determined to make time for your work, you should delegate responsibility for other matters to someone else and only accept an interruption if the crisis is something that that other person cannot deal with.

The work took longer than anticipated

If you work to the rule that any piece of work will always take longer than you think, unless it is so routine that you can estimate the time it will take with accuracy, then you will always have enough time in which to complete it. Some jobs will take longer, others will take less time then expected, and the result will be that you have contingency time built in to your work schedule.

Some managers never seem to have enough time. They are always running just to keep up, and the result will be increasing stress that can eventually result in mental and physical illness. If you are one of those managers, or even feel you have a tendency to become one, some of the ideas outlined below (and summarised in Checklist 1.7) may help you to save time in general. You may also find them helpful as advice to give to members of your staff who seem to have difficulties managing their time.

Checklist 1.7   Time savers

- Clear your desk.
- Plan for the day ahead.
- Organise others.
- Be ruthless about meetings.

Clear your desk

Some managers seem to thrive in a chaos of paperwork but, in reality, they are probably sinking beneath its weight. You cannot lay your hands on an essential piece of paper if it is 'filed' somewhere amidst a great pile of other papers. Instead, you waste your valuable time searching for it – often in vain.

If your desk is hidden beneath an uncontrolled heap of loose papers, the first thing you have to do is set aside some time to clear it. It is probable that much of it can be thrown away. If you haven't read that article you promised yourself you would by now, then you probably never will. So you can throw it out or, at least keep a file for 'Articles to be read'. If filing is not one of your strengths, you may have a secretary who would take this on for you – but it would have to be on a regular basis, say once a week at least.

'Never pick up a piece of paper without doing something with it' is a useful piece of advice. And 'doing something with it' includes throwing it in the bin as well as replying to it, filing it or acting upon it.

Plan for the day ahead

You can either do this the day before or come in early and make your plan before starting work. I prefer to do this the day before, stopping that day's work at least 15 minutes before leaving the office and thinking about what needs to be done the next day. First, make a list of the jobs you know have to be done, for example:

- write report for Management Group
- write up Sheila's appraisal

- see Max about the problems with Tancam
- fix up an appointment with Alison
- finish the accommodation survey
- talk to Greg about his time keeping
- attend Lou's retirement get-together

Once you have noted down the things that have to be done tomorrow, put them in order of importance by noting down a number against each item, starting with '1' for the most important. Then, bearing in mind that everything takes longer than you think, allocate a realistic period of time against each one. Add your times up and add some time for lunch and *one hour of 'free' time* for the things that might crop up. If your total comes to more hours than you are expected to work, then go through your list and either postpone one or more less important jobs or consider whether or not they could be delegated to someone else. Leave the list in the middle of your – clear – desk so that it is the first thing you see in the morning. Then, follow your plan through. Resist being diverted from your priorities, and you may even find you can go home early that night – and every night.

Organise others

Delegation is part of the subject matter of Chapter 7 and is very important. Delegating doesn't just mean telling, or asking, someone else to do something for you; it involves explaining what needs to be done, how it needs to be done and when it needs to be done. It also involves delegating to the right person – someone who is capable of taking over that task and performing it competently.

You also need to allocate work to your staff in such a way that what they are expected to do is feasible and they have adequate resources for doing the work – including time. Ask them for feedback on how the work is progressing so that you will know if what you have asked someone to do is possible, and possible within a certain timescale.

Be ruthless about meetings

Meetings can be great time wasters in that they can tie up the valuable time of a number of people, including yourself. In the next chapter, we look at effective ways of running meetings, but you may have to attend meetings that you don't set up yourself and over which you have little or no control. Sometimes, it is organisationally necessary to take part in these meetings for your own career advancement or for the well-being of your department. Where this is not the case, weigh up the pros and cons of attending meetings in which you take little part, discuss matters that are not of value to you or your department, never make decisions, or that go on for hours. Is this a good use of your time?

➡ MANAGING STRESS

Stress was mentioned in the last section as resulting from the mismanagement of time. That is one reason for stress but, of course, there are others. For example, you or a member of your staff may have problems outside the work situation that are affecting the ability to concentrate and are creating stress. Or you may have been given, or given someone else, a task that they cannot possibly undertake, either through lack of ability or training or through lack of adequate resources. Stress can also be caused by poor working conditions such as unacceptable noise levels, too warm or too cold an atmosphere, cramped working space, unpleasant work colleagues, harassment, discrimination and so on. It can also be caused by fear – fear of losing your job, of not doing the job well, of not being promoted, of not making enough money.

Stress is on the increase at all levels in organisations. It can cost an employer dearly in terms of hours lost through stress-related illnesses and in compensation where stress at work can be proved to be the cause for prolonged ill-health or unemployment.

Go through Checklist 1.8, which gives a list of common signs of stress, and see if you can identify any of the signs in yourself or in any of the people for whom you are responsible.

Checklist 1.8 **Common signs of stress**

- irritability
- feeling bored
- loss of appetite or overeating
- feeling tired without good reason
- lack of concentration
- increase in smoking
- increase in drinking alcohol
- frequent headaches
- poor timekeeping
- persistent absenteeism
- difficulty in sleeping
- anger towards work colleagues

There are a number of other factors that can induce stress at work, related to the job itself, and these are listed in Checklist 1.9. Go through the checklist, thinking about the jobs of the people who work for you, and consider whether any of these factors might be present in their jobs. Is there any relationship between anyone who is demonstrating signs of stress and any of the job factors listed in Checklist 1.9?

Checklist 1.9 **Causes of job stress**

- little or no freedom over decisions or plans related to their work (low job discretion)
- low use of skills
- low or high work demands, including intellectual and physical demands
- repetitive, monotonous work with very little variety
- no knowledge or feedback about how well they are performing
- uncertainty about the future of the job and/or the organisation
- low pay
- poor working conditions

- doing a job seen as of little value in society

  (adapted from P. Warr, 1992)

Preventing and managing stress at work

Some stress at work is unavoidable and, indeed, can be beneficial. We are talking here about 'excessive stress' – the kind of stress that leads to illness. And this kind of stress should be prevented whenever possible.

As a manager, you may not have very much control over the jobs your staff are required to perform, but you may be able to increase job discretion. Warr sees low job discretion as the single factor most likely to cause excessive stress in individuals. Job discretion is the giving to the individual of more control over the work that is being done and more responsibility. Can that person work without constant supervision and checking up to see that the job is being done correctly, for example? Can the job be enhanced by combining it with other related jobs and re-allocating work amongst several people?

As far as some of the other job-related stress factors are concerned, you might be able to introduce job rotation so that one person is not always performing the same repetitive, boring job but has a chance to perform other tasks. You can certainly provide feedback on performance – indeed, this should be one of your tasks as a manager as you will see in Chapters 2 and 5. And you may be able to do something about poor working conditions, particularly if they contravene the Health and Safety regulations. You probably can do little about low pay, but there may be other rewards you can offer such as praise or increased responsibility through delegation. Motivation and rewards will be discussed in detail in Chapter 4 and you might like to move on to that chapter after finishing this one if you feel stress at work is a major problem.

If you feel you are suffering from excessive stress yourself, first try to determine the reason for this. Always look for the root cause, whether it is work-related, domestic or from some other source. This, then, is the area of your life that needs to be changed in some way to reduce your stress level.

You may need to seek professional advice or therapeutic help.

Relaxation and meditation, for example, are proven methods of reducing tension and stress, but they don't remove the cause. They may, however, enable you to accept more readily certain aspects of your working or domestic life, thus making them less stressful, or to recognise what it is that is causing the stress and what you might be able to do about reducing it.

➡ MANAGING YOUR MANAGER AND MANAGING WITH OTHER MANAGERS

No manager, apart from owner–managers of very small businesses, manage in a vacuum. Managers have managers to manage them, apart from the most senior management. And managers need to work with other managers to get things done.

Most managers are promoted because they are successful and good managers of people and other resources. But there are exceptions. You may be fortunate enough to work for a manager who respects you for who you are and what you do, who provides you with advice and help when you need it, offers you training and development opportunities, gives you feedback on how you are performing and generally acts as your mentor and guide. Or you may work for someone who does none of these things. What can you do if this happens?

Depending on the management structure of your organisation, you could go above your manager if you feel you have true grounds for complaint, but you would need to ensure you could demonstrate that your manager was ineffective and not just offer anecdotal and subjective evidence. To do this, you have to start ensuring that all your dealings with your manager are recorded in writing since any complaint you take to a higher level may well turn into a formal grievance.

Try to find out if your manager behaves in the same way to your colleagues and other managers – or is it possibly an interpersonal problem between the two of you? Do you irritate your manager, for example? Is some of the fault on your side? Try talking to your manager. Your relationship may be the result of misunderstandings in the past, which one or both of you had not recognised. Try to find an opportunity to put your point of view, without losing your temper or descending into wild accusations.

If all else fails, you may need to ask for a transfer or even leave the organisation, since poor interpersonal relationships of this type can cause considerable stress at work.

Managing with other managers involves networking – spending time getting to know other managers in the organisation, the jobs they do, their areas of expertise. This is usually a fairly informal process, although you may have opportunities to meet other managers on certain organisational occasions. Knowing the strengths of other managers means that you can call upon them when you need their help or advice – and they can call on you in return.

Some of you may have shared interests outside work, which can often facilitate good working relationships. Here, however, there is a danger that women managers are excluded from such networks because, for example, they don't necessarily play the same sports as men, are less likely to go drinking after work and have different outside interests. It is still true in most of the world today that male managers significantly outnumber women managers and that the organisational networks that are set up are predominantly male. There are often too few women managers for them to form a predominantly female network even if they wanted to.

One way of overcoming the 'male-dominated network' syndrome is for the organisation, or its managers, to make formalised opportunities for all its managers to meet and discuss what is going on in their particular areas, what help or resources they could use and what experience and expertise they could offer to other managers. Interdepartmental staff training sessions, for example, are one way of harnessing internal organisational expertise.

However, all this, once again, involves time – time to get to know other managers, to establish a network, and to meet other managers. Only you can decide whether time spent in this way is productive for you, for your staff and for the organisation as a whole.

➡ **CHRIS'S PROBLEM (1)**

Chris has had a bad day. It started with a traffic jam on the motorway, which meant arriving at work a good half-hour later than usual. Then Jenny, one of the staff in another department, had complained to her manager that Chris had been rude to her. The manager had sent a memo, pointing out that this wasn't the first time someone had complained to her about Chris being rude or short-tempered with members of staff. Chris was already late for a meeting and had to go without the papers for it as they couldn't be found. The meeting went on for about two hours and Chris got more and more annoyed with the Chair, who couldn't seem to control what was going on – or, rather what was not going on because discussion just went round and round in circles and no one came up with any ideas or decisions for improving the situation.

When the meeting finished, it was too late for lunch but Chris wasn't hungry anyway and had far too much work to catch up on. There were eight telephone calls to return, eleven e-mails to respond to and an urgent report to write, which should have been with the Marketing Director two days ago. There was also a message from Don, one of the supervisors, asking for a quick word. Chris knew all about Don's words; they were anything but 'quick'. There simply wasn't time to see him today. Chris could feel a headache starting but, before being able to get down to all the work that needed to be done, the Head of Department came into the office.

'Chris, I need someone to go down to Exeter this afternoon. I'm playing golf and I can't put it off so I'll get Marie to give you the directions. You'll need to be there by 4 o'clock and you've to see Godfrey Houghton about the Patterton business. I know you don't know much about it, but neither does he.'

You go into see Chris just as the Head of Department is leaving and Chris pours out all the troubles of the day to you. What advice would you give Chris?

References

British Institute of Management (Cannon and Taylor Working Party Report), *Management Development to the Millennium* (BIM, London, 1994)

Fayol H., *General and Industrial Management* (Pitman, London, 1949)

The Personnel Manager's Factbook (1997)

Hunt J. W., *Managing People at Work*, 2nd ed. (McGraw-Hill Book Co (UK) Ltd, Berkshire, 1986)

Steel, Sir David, in R. Wild, *How to Manage* (1992) p. 34

Tannenbaum R. and Schmidt W., 'How to choose a leadership pattern' in *Harvard Business Review*, March–April 1958

Warr P., 'Job features and excessive stress' in R. Jenkins and N. Coney (eds), *Prevention of Mental Ill-health at Work* (HMSO, Norwich, 1992)

Chapter 2
Talking to people

'Gobbledygook is the methodology deployed by governmental bureaucracies specifically designed to ensure that the simplest of instructions is encased in a plethora of treacherous subclauses, adverbial phrases and cross references, with the result that the recipient is left baffled, bemused and confused.'

(Cutts and Maher, 1984)

I don't imagine, once you have unravelled the above quotation from *Gobbledygook*, that you would disagree with what it says. There is a tendency in bureaucratic organisations of all kinds, not just governmental ones, to use several words where one would do and to ensure those words have as many syllables as possible. The result, as the authors of *Gobbledygook* point out, is that people have considerable difficulty in understanding what has been written. Think how impossible it must be if such writing is not in your first language!

Equally confusing is when people speak or write in their own shorthand and expect you to understand it: 'I went to G and M today to see about the sprogs for the TF converter – can you find out where they are?' Well, you might if you knew what they were. ...

Then there is jargon. Like the shorthand used in the example just given, this can be easily understood if you work in the same organisational area. But it can be a form of secret language that excludes everyone else. Lawyers and doctors are particularly prone to using a professional jargon, but it happens in other organisations as well.

There are a number of ways that we communicate with each other in a work situation and Checklist 2.1 below lists some of these, their benefits and their limitations. As you go through, consider how many of these methods you use in your organisation.

Checklist 2.1 Methods of communication at work

Method	Benefits	Limitations
Noticeboards	Quick and cheap	Must be up-to-date; should not be used for sensitive information
Meetings	Provide two-way communication; everyone has a chance to contribute	Can be time-wasting
Reports; memos	Permanent record; can be used for confidential/ sensitive communications	Increases paperwork
Corridor conversations	Useful for keeping in touch informally with what is happening	No record normally kept
Information points	Available to all	Dependent on space
Newsletters	Engender commitment	Selective information; may be produced for a number of different audiences
Electronic mail	Quick; cuts down on paper	Cannot be retrieved once sent

➡ **TALKING WITH PEOPLE FACE-TO-FACE**

I am going to start by looking at how we communicate in person to other people, before going on to discuss other forms of communication. If you found the paragraph from *Gobbledygook* incomprehensible to start with, just imagine how difficult it can be when people *speak* like that.

Talking to one other

Managing people involves talking to them, often in a one-to-one situation. You may have instructions to give them, questions to ask, an appraisal to carry out and so on. But are you always sure that the other person has understood what you have been saying? Often, especially if you are in a hurry or if you assume that the other person has some knowledge that they do not in fact possess, your spoken message can be distorted. Equally often, the other person, particularly if they are in a subordinate position to you, may be nervous about asking for clarification – they don't want to appear foolish or ignorant. As a result, you have a communication breakdown.

Think of face-to-face communication of this kind as an exchange between a Sender and Receiver. The person who is speaking is the Sender; the person who is listening is the Receiver. The Receiver has to 'decode' what the Sender is saying in order to understand the message. In conversation, these roles will alternate. However, as we saw from the preceding paragraph, this doesn't always work. Checklist 2.2 notes some barriers to effective communication. Think about an occasion when face-to-face communication didn't work, when you were Sender or Receiver, and try to identify which barrier(s) caused the breakdown.

| Checklist 2.2 | Barriers to communication |

- inappropriate language (gobbledygook, jargon, acronyms, poor English or non-English)
- information overload (too much information for the Receiver to take in)
- information underload (too little information)

- noise or other distractions
- different perspectives (Sender and Receiver view the subject matter from opposing perspectives)
- a failure to listen to the message
- deliberate deception (the Receiver is holding something back)
- receiver's mind on something else (doesn't decode the full message)

Feedback

One of the ways of avoiding such barriers to communication is through giving or asking for feedback on what has been said. Feedback is a process of checking and clarifying what has actually been said by the other person. It can involve asking questions, asking for the message to be repeated or repeating it yourself. The objective of feedback is to ensure that both the Sender and Receiver understand the same message.

As a manager, it should be you that takes the initiative in the feedback process. Look at the two examples below.

Example 1a

MANAGER: Kaz, I want you to go to the store and bring back 150 thostles. You'll need to take an order form with you – Yasmin has those. Take them to Ben in Purchasing and make sure you get a receipt from him, which you need to give to someone in Sales. OK?

KAZ: OK.

And Kaz, who has only been in the job for a week, goes off to the store, forgets the order form and has to go back for it, can't remember who he has to see in Purchasing and forgets entirely about the receipt. A lot of time has been wasted and, with no receipt, the order will probably be lost in the system. Multiply such mistakes severalfold, and the organisation will be losing money. It will probably lose Kaz as well, because he will become frustrated and anxious that he isn't doing his job properly. Let's look at some ways in which that particular situation might have been improved through feedback.

Example 1b

MANAGER: Kaz, I want you to go down to the store and bring back 150 thostles. You know what thostles are?

KAZ: Yes, those small springs we use in making up the winding mechanisms.

MANAGER: That's right. We need 150 of them. Go and see Yasmin and tell her you need an order form for them. Do you know Yasmin?

KAZ: No, I've never met her.

MANAGER: She's in the office next to mine. You know where the store is, don't you?

KAZ: Oh yes, I've been there several times.

MANAGER: Fine. Once you've got the thostles, take them over to Ben in Purchasing – do you know where that is?

KAZ: No, I've never been there.

MANAGER: Well, it's not difficult. It's right next to the store. If you have any problems, ask someone to point you in the right direction. Ben will be at the main desk and you need a receipt from him for the thostles. Then take the receipt to Sales, which is upstairs from Purchasing. Give it to whoever is on the desk there. Now that's a rather complicated job especially as you're new here. Would you like to go through it so we both know what needs to be done?

KAZ: Yes, I've to get an order form from Yasmin for 150 thostles, take it to the store and pick them up. Then I take the thostles to Ben in Purchasing and get a receipt from him, which I give to whoever is on the desk in Sales.

MANAGER: That's it, Kaz. Well done. Off you go then.

By breaking down the instructions and asking Kaz for feedback on his understanding at every stage, the manager in that example has ensured he understands what needs to be done. It took a little longer than the manager's instructions in the first example, but very little extra time compared with the time that Kaz might have wasted in getting everything wrong.

Listening

One of the barriers to communication is a failure to listen. Often we make assumptions about what the other person is saying, 'switch off' and start thinking about something else. People who are under stress or are angry about something, often don't listen at all – you are bound to have heard two people shouting at each other but completely failing to hear what the other person is trying to say. Or the speaker is so boring and long-winded that the listener's thoughts drift off what is being said.

As a Receiver, you can practise 'active' listening. As its name suggests, it is not a passive part of the communication process and involves your participation because you want to collect accurate information from the Sender. There are three kinds of active listening that managers can employ for different purposes.

- support listening
- responding listening
- retention listening

Support listening involves encouraging the Sender to tell you more so that you can find out what they think or feel. It is the kind of listening employed by counsellors and therapists – and by managers when their staff appear to have a problem. You can encourage the Sender to say more through nods and smiles, putting the person at ease, and by occasionally asking the Sender to enlarge on something he or she has already said. However, your aim is to get the Sender to say more, not to say too much yourself.

Responding listening is more conversational and involves asking questions for clarification or responding to questions from the Sender. Retention listening is used when you need to gather factual information.

Non-verbal communication

So far, we have been looking at the things people say. But equally important, and sometimes more important, are the things that are not spoken but that are communicated through facial expressions, gestures, body posture and so on – the non-verbal clues to what the speaker is really feeling and thinking. Checklist 2.3 gives a list of different kinds of non-verbal clues, which are discussed in detail below.

Checklist 2.3 **Non-verbal communication clues**

- touch and touch-avoidance
- physical space
- posture
- physical appearance
- facial expression
- eye contact and gaze
- gesture
- voice tone and pitch
- silence
- speech errors
- accent

Some of these clues tell us something about the person who is speaking, particularly if we have never met them before. Physical appearance – clothing, hair style, tidiness or untidiness – all tell us something about the individual. Beware, however, of jumping to conclusions; these are only clues and need facts to support them. If you are an untidy person who never cares much about what clothes you wear, you would probably react more favourably to another person who had a similar appearance than to someone who seemed to be excessively neat and tidy. Accent, too, can give us a clue as to where the person comes from geographically.

Touch or touch-avoidance can be a cultural clue in that, in some cultures, constantly touching another person is a natural way of communicating. The British, for example, usually avoid touching another person unless they know them very well. In France, people from Marseilles may touch each other quite a number of times during a conversation, whereas Parisians are similar to the British. The British or Parisian manager observing two people who touched each other relatively frequently might infer – wrongly, perhaps – that they had a very close relationship.

Physical space can be a clue to both culture and status. Think of the judge on a bench or the speaker on a platform. The physical space between them and others is quite considerable and reflects status and importance. Personal space – that is, the distance between you and the person you are talking to – is usually around 1.2 metres but Germans, North Americans and Swedes tend to prefer a greater distance while Latin Americans, Greeks, southern Italians and Arabs need less. Invasion of this personal space can create problems in communication since, if you get closer to a person than they like, that person can become quite agitated and concerned, and then communication falters.

Posture, gestures, facial expression, eye contact and gaze can all give clues to what the person is thinking, as can the tone or pitch of the voice – and silence. The way a person sits or stands can be an indication of how relaxed or otherwise they are with the conversation. Some facial expressions are hard to control, such as blushing or registering surprise or amusement. We tend to look for these clues subconsciously and have difficulty in relating to people who are relatively expressionless. Eye contact also seems to be a necessary adjunct to communication – it shows us that the person is interested in what we are saying. Lack of eye contact or gaze in a speaker often means they are unhappy about what they are saying or that what they are saying is untrue.

Gestures can be very powerful clues. If you don't speak a particular language, using gestures to mime what you want can be very effective. The way a person uses their hands, in particular, can be a clue to how they are feeling. Are their gestures expansive, showing enthusiasm or anger or excitement? Or are they tightly clasped, possibly indicating grief or unhappiness or excessive stress? The tone and pitch of the voice can signal that the person is getting excited or upset – high pitch, staccato tone – or is having difficulties with what they have to say – tone is slower, pitch lower. Of course, you need to decode these clues to get the right message!

Silence worries some people; they feel they have to jump in and talk to fill it. A speaker may use it deliberately so as to make the next point more powerful, to create tension or to buy time in order to think of a response to what has been said. It can be a sign of confidence in some, of nervousness and an inability to respond in others. Speech errors such as slips of the tongue, misuse of words, leaving sentences unfinished can also be a sign of nervousness.

Next time you have a chance to observe two people in conversation, particularly if you don't know them, look for the non-verbal clues to their character and behaviour.

Talking to, and in, groups

Making presentations to groups of people, however well you know them, can be very daunting, but the adrenaline they cause can also be very useful. When you are making a presentation, you are a performer. You have to ensure that you get your main message across, using whatever media are most appropriate, and that you gain the interest of your audience. The secret of successful presentations is preparation.

Checklist 2.4 is concerned with questions you should ask yourself or someone else before making a presentation.

Checklist 2.4   What is the presentation aiming to do?

- Why am I making this presentation (and not someone else)?
- Where will I be making it?
- Who will I be making it to?
- How many will be in the audience?
- How much do they know about the topic?
- What kind of presentation is it to be?
- How long have I got?
- Will that time include questions from the audience?
- Is the topic likely to be controversial?
- Will I need other experts with me to answer technical questions?

It is important for you to know who will be listening to your presentation because it enables you to pitch it at the right level. Obviously, a presentation to people who know nothing about the topic will need much more background information than one to a knowledgeable audience. You need to know how long you have got and whether to expect questions or whether yours is only one of a number of presentations. You also need to be clear about whether you are 'selling' something – a product, an idea, a change – or giving information about it; these kinds of presentations need different approaches. And you need to know whether it is likely to be controversial in case you have to answer awkward questions – which may be where you need assistance.

Having got the answers to the questions in Checklist 2.4, you need to think about how to structure your presentation. Ideally, it should have a beginning, a middle and an end and it should clearly and concisely get your message across to your audience. Some people like to start with, or bring in, a joke or two, but usually this isn't necessary (nor advisable unless you are very good at telling relevant jokes). Avoid, at all costs jokes that are sexist, racist or offensive in any way; they will alienate part of your audience immediately. Wit is so much cleverer than jokes.

Checklist 2.5 gives you one way of designing a structure for your presentation.

Checklist 2.5   Structuring a presentation

(1) Introduction

(2) The present position

(3) The current problem or opportunity

(4) The possible solutions

(5) Your recommendations

(6) Conclusion

You need some kind of introduction that sets out, briefly, what you are going to be talking about. You also need to outline the present position, in more detail to an audience who know very little about it. Follow this with a clear outline of the problem or opportunity facing you, your audience or the organisation as a whole, ensuring that they really understand what it is before offering some options or possible solutions. You will probably have a preferred option and you can 'sell' this quite cleverly through listing the benefits and disadvantages of all options, your preference having more benefits than disadvantages! But you need to be sure that you are not underselling the other options that you don't really want to have to implement, or you might create a backlash. Having put forward your own recommendation (or that of a group you have been working with), bring the presentation to a close by summarising what you have said.

Presentations usually involve more than a person standing up and speaking to an audience and you may want to use visual aids to make your point. These may be overhead projection transparencies, computerised graphics or even a simple flip chart or chalkboard. Whatever type of visual aid you use, keep it simple. Nothing is more distracting or infuriating than a slide so packed with information that you cannot read it, and it detracts from what you are saying. Checklist 2.6 suggests the next stage of preparation – finding out about the place in which you are going to be making your presentation.

| Checklist 2.6 | **Preparing the place** |

- How big is the room?
- Will there be a microphone if necessary?
- How will the audience be seated?
- What visual aid equipment is available?
- What visual aid equipment could I bring in if necessary?
- When can I check that the equipment is working and how to work it?
- Will everyone be able to see me and my visual aids?
- Is the lighting too strong/too weak?
- Can the lighting be changed if necessary?
- Is there a table for my notes?
- What should I wear?

And don't do as I did when making a presentation to the Confederation of British Industries and trust someone else with your notes and slides. They were sitting on his desk 50 miles away when I discovered he didn't have them, ten minutes before I was due to speak. My only recourse was to ask my audience for sympathy and, while it was one of the best-received presentations I had ever made, I would certainly not recommend it in terms of stress level!

Meetings

> 'A committee is a cul-de-sac down which ideas are lured and then quietly strangled.' (Cocks, 1973)

I mentioned the potentially time-wasting aspects of meetings in Chapter 1, particularly if they are unproductive or go on for too long. But it is difficult for managers to avoid meetings and, very often, it is the manager who calls the meetings and takes the chair. Running an effective meeting is a skill, and one that is much valued. Checklist 2.7 lists the commonest kinds of formal meetings held in organisations. As you go through it, try to identify which of the meetings described you attend or lead.

Checklist 2.7   Formal meetings

- briefing meetings – to give information and instructions, responding to questions
- business meetings – for making business-related decisions
- planning meetings/working groups – for planning events, developing policy, programming work etc
- consultation meetings – between senior and junior staff, management and trade unions, to increase involvement and information
- staff meetings – to report on developments or to discuss issues of common interest

You could ask the question 'Why, with all the advances in communication technology, do we need to hold meetings anyway?' True, teleconferencing can replace the need for everyone to be in the same place, but it still takes up meeting time. Some issues can be dealt with more effectively through electronic mail or conferencing systems but, in general, well-run face-to-face meetings:

- engender a sense of involvement
- are consistent with a democratic style of management
- facilitate communication amongst all levels of staff
- improve decision making by involving a range of viewpoints
- keep managers in touch with what is going on in the organisation

Running meetings

As with making presentations, running meetings (and participating in them) requires preparation. Checklist 2.8 offers a number of areas where preparation for meetings will ensure that they run as smoothly and as effectively as possible. As you go through the checklist, imagine you are about to run a meeting, or think of a meeting you have chaired recently; do you make these kind of preparations beforehand? The timescales are only suggested ones for meetings that take place about once a month; obviously, for weekly or fortnightly meetings; the timescales would need to be shorter.

Checklist 2.8   **Preparing for meetings**

- One week after the last meeting:
  - ensure the minutes or notes of the last meeting have been written up and sent out
  - ensure everyone knows the date of the next meeting
- Two weeks before the next meeting:
  - ask members for suggestions for the agenda
  - ask for any papers for the meeting to be written and sent to you within one week
- One week before the meeting:
  - construct and send out the agenda
  - send out a note calling the meeting and giving the date, time and place
  - ask members to let you know if they cannot attend
  - invite any non-members whom you would like to attend for particular items
  - arrange for any papers to be copied and sent out in advance

- arrange for any briefing you may need on any topics on the agenda
- read all the papers yourself and make notes about any issues you would like to raise
- ensure arrangements have been made for tea/coffee lunch etc

• The day before the meeting:
  - check who is coming to the meeting
  - allocate rough timings to each item on the agenda
  - decide which items need decisions

• The day of the meeting:
  - start on time even if everyone expected is not present
  - try to keep to your timings on the agenda
  - let everyone have their say
  - don't let individuals take over the meeting or repeat themselves
  - prompt members to make decisions where necessary
  - try and finish on time
  - check the date of the next meeting with those present

It may be your job to write up the minutes but, if you are also the Chair, this can be very difficult. In those circumstances, ask for a volunteer to take notes so that you can give your full attention to the business of the meeting.

If you are not running the meeting but participating in it, you also have a responsibility to ensure you read all the papers so that you can participate fully. There is nothing more time-wasting and infuriating than people at meetings who have obviously not read the papers and who are asking questions that are answered in those papers. You also have a responsibility to let the Chair know in advance if there is a particular subject you want to be discussed. In many formal meetings, the Chair will refuse to add items to the agenda unless he or she has been informed about them in advance.

You can also help the meeting to run smoothly by ensuring you have prepared what you want to say and by asking for views from valued members. In fact, it is often a good idea to discuss what you

want to say beforehand with one or more of the people who will
be attending the meeting so that you can incorporate their ideas.

➡ WRITTEN COMMUNICATION

An awful lof of paper seems to circulate around organisations –
memos, reports, notes, letters and so on. Checklist 2.9 lists these
types of written communication, and as you go through it, identify
the kinds that you send and receive as a manager.

Checklist 2.9 **Written communication**

- memos
- replies to memos
- letters
- replies to letters
- notes
- replies to notes
- formal reports
- informal reports
- comments on reports
- discussion papers
- summaries of other written documents
- minutes or meeting notes
- project proposals
- budgets
- tenders
- policy papers
- procedure documents
- conference papers
- press releases
- electronic mail printouts
- publicity/advertising copy

- instructional material

(from *The Effective Manager*, 1996)

All this written material takes time to compose, takes time to respond to, and takes up space on your desk or in a filing cabinet. Is it all necessary? The answer is probably 'No.' Yet organisations continue to produce paperwork.

In some cases, a telephone call or a visit could replace paper (although many managers then send a follow-up note or memo, recording what was discussed or agreed). Electronic mail was supposed to bring about the 'paperless office'; in fact, there is evidence to show it creates more paperwork. Many people would argue, rightly, that something that is written down is formalised and can be used as evidence. This is certainly necessary in cases of grievance or complaint, or where someone is being warned about having committed a disciplinary offence.

Written communication is usually essential in the following cases:

- if the information is complex
- if the information needs to be retained
- if the information needs to be acted on
- when it is important there are no future misunderstandings about what was said

Rigorous filing and de-filing (getting rid of out-of-date papers) is one way of keeping the paperwork under control. There are other ways such as:

- delegating some of your writing tasks to an assistant or secretary
- composing standard letters to reply to routine correspondence
- dictating memos or letters to someone willing to key them in

However you choose a deal with your paperwork, you are still going to have to write some things and, as with face-to-face communication, you will need to write them in such a way that the recipient understands. To do this, you should follow the guidelines in Checklist 2.10.

Checklist 2.10 Guidelines for written communication

- Have a structure to what you write.
- Avoid long words and sentences.
- Avoid jargon.
- Think about the simplest way in which you could say what you want.
- Ensure that when you use words such as 'this' and 'it', your recipient will be clear as to what these refer to.
- Use punctuation correctly.
- Use an appropriate format – e.g. don't start a report with 'Dear John'.

Below are two examples of business writing, both from Giles and Hedge (1994). Although they are both attempting to say the same thing, one is a poor example and the other is good.

Example 2

Because the training department has invested in the provision of language teaching, over 30% of the company's managers are now able to communicate at a survival level with their European counterparts in French or German and this has improved collaboration between the French, German and UK companies to such an extent that the training department has now been given a further £30,000 for additional language courses.

Example 3

The training department has trained 30% of the company's managers to commmunicate at survival level with their French or German counterparts. This has improved collaboration between French, German and UK companies. As a result, the training department has been given a further £30,000 for additional language courses.

The second example is better than the first, mainly because it uses shorter sentences, which allows the reader to take in a manageable amount of information at a time. When in doubt, shorten your sentences.

Report writing

Most managers have to write reports about or for their staff. Some organisations have a strict format in which all reports must be written; this is a discipline and certainly ensures all necessary areas have been covered. In general, however, reports should include the items given in Checklist 2.11.

Checklist 2.11 Contents and structure of a written report

- a title, author's name and date of writing
- a summary – written at the end but placed at the beginning
- an introduction
- the main body of the report, using numbered sections, headings and sub-headings
- conclusions
- recommendations
- appendices (for appropriate data, evidence etc.), where inclusion in the main body of text would detract from the flow

Each part of the report should be headed appropriately, such as 'Summary', 'Recommendations' etc. Any numbering system can be used, so long as it is used consistently. (Some report writers number every paragraph and this can be very helpful when referring to an item in the body of the report as being in '... paragraph 3.1' for example.)

When you have finished any piece of writing, but reports in particular, try to read it over as if you were the receiver not the sender. Ask yourself the questions in Checklist 2.12 as you do so.

Checklist 2.12 Questions to ask of your written communication

- Does it make sense?

- Are there too many, or superfluous, words?
- Are the sentences short?
- Is the language simple?
- Is the format appropriate?
- Have I made it clear what I want to say or what action I want taken?

➡ ELECTRONIC COMMUNICATION

Various forms of electronic communication are widely used nowadays both inside and outside organisations, of which the most common are word processing, electronic mail and conferencing. However, using the telephone is also a form of electronic communication.

The telephone is often the first point of contact for customers and clients, and the way it is answered is important to the image of your organisation. It is also widely used to contact people inside and outside the organisation when you want an immediate conversation. It has the advantage of connecting two people instantly without physical disturbance, but it has the disadvantage that it relies on voice alone and there are few non-verbal clues.

Word processing is now so common that it has replaced handwriting. It has the advantages of moving text around, being able to delete and change text, checking for spelling and grammar and providing synonyms. It can produce numerous different layouts, fonts and typescripts, which enhance the appearance of the document, and it is a distinct improvement on poor handwriting! It also means that large amounts of text can be stored on floppy discs, which are easy to store and transport.

Electronic mail is a communication tool whereby managers and others on the same (or an interlinked) system can exchange information electronically. It is particularly useful for sending information quickly to a large number of people, using a circulation list, and for replying instantly to messages using the 'Reply' function. However, there are also dangers with the system in that, once sent, a message cannot be retrieved. This means that if you dash off a message in anger or in haste, it can have a negative effect on the receiver.

Electronic mail can be useful for sending confidential information, since an individual's 'mailbox' can only, in theory, be accessed by that person through a password. However, no computer system is impenetrable and you only have to write down or tell someone your password for others to be able to read your mail. In fact, you don't even need to do that since your mailbox can be infiltrated by a computer 'hacker' if he or she really wants to read your mail. There is also the increased danger of causing offence, particularly if you send a message in the heat of the moment. I know of at least two cases which may well come to an industrial tribunal or to law because of defamatory remarks made in an electronic mail message.

Computer conferencing is not as widely used as electronic mail but serves a similar purpose. In conferencing, the computer acts like a notice board on which people put messages and others respond to them with their own messages. This can lead to an (albeit stilted) 'conversation' between a number of people with similar interests or work objectives. Videoconferencing, on the other hand, brings back the visual clues to electronic communication since you can see the other person or persons as you speak to them. Both these forms of computer-mediated communication are discussed in more detail in Chapter 8.

➡ **CHRIS'S PROBLEM (2)**

Chris had been asked to make a presentation about the work of the department and has just returned looking very depressed.

'How did it go?' you ask, although you immediately wish you hadn't.

'It was a disaster,' replies Chris. 'Everything that could go wrong went wrong. They hadn't told me it was a presentation to senior management so I just went along in my everyday clothes, nothing smart or anything like that. It was a huge room and you know I've got a soft voice so the ones at the back couldn't hear me. Then the overhead projector went bust on me – I just couldn't get the thing to work so I couldn't use my slides and that put me off. I even lost my place a couple of times – my notes had got out of order. And then, as if that wasn't bad enough, old Trudgett came up to me at the end and told me off for being casual about things like presentations and meetings. Apparently he hadn't got the papers for the meeting tomorrow and he didn't know where it was being held or anything. Blamed me because I'm the Chair, but it's Clare's job to get the papers and things out, not mine.'

What advice could you offer Chris about making presentations and running meetings?

References

Cocks B., *New Scientist*, November 1973

Cutts M. and Maher C., *Gobbledygook* (1984)

Giles K. and Hedge N., *The Manager's Good Study Guide* (Open University, Milton Keynes, 1994)

The Effective Manager (Open University Business School, Milton Keynes, 1996)

Chapter 3
Making decisions and plans

'It is harder to change a decision than to make one.'

(Anon)

What do you think about the quotation above? Have you experienced times when you have made a wrong or poor decision and then found it difficult to change? You might argue that, for example, if you decide to order a new word processor and then change your mind, that decision is relatively simple to reverse unless you have entered into some kind of written agreement with the supplier. But decisions that directly involve other people can be more difficult to change. If you decide to appoint someone to a new post, or promote a junior member of your staff, or change the content of someone's job, these are important decisions that affect other people and reversing them can be complex.

Managers make decisions all the time, some of them routine, some of them complicated. They also make plans that involve decision making. For example, even something as apparently simple as drawing up a holiday rota involves you in deciding who can and will take holidays at certain periods and whether you need to cover for absent staff by redeploying existing people or by employing temporary staff. Planning a large project obviously takes more time and more complex decision-making skills.

In this chapter, you will be looking first at how, as a manager, you make decisions before going on to look at some planning techniques.

➡ MAKING DECISIONS

I have already hinted at the difference between making simple, routine decisions and making more complex ones. The former are the kinds of decisions you barely think about before making them, such as closing the door to prevent a draught, turning on the light so that you can see what you are reading, lifting the telephone when it rings. You may not even think of these actions as decisions, but they are *because they involve choice* – you could choose to leave the door open, to stop reading or to ignore the ring of the telephone. Other simple decisions are those that you have made many times before or that have a well worked-out procedure to follow, such as processing a sales order or working with a computer spreadsheet. Herbert Simon, an American professor who was awarded the Nobel Prize for Economics, describes such simple, routine decisions as 'programmed' in that you don't have to think about them afresh each time you make them. There is, of course, a danger that programmed decisions are not always correct or appropriate and that they become erroneously embedded into the routine.

The other kinds of decisions, the more complex ones, Simon refers to as 'non-programmed' because they are unfamiliar, difficult, complicated and unstructured. This does not mean that, within a non-programmed decision, there would not be programmed sub-decisions. For example, take planning a major new project. Although this would involve many non-programmed decisions because the issue was complex and unfamiliar, it would also involve programmed decisions where procedures could be followed or where you had experience of decision making in the past.

Checklist 3.1 below gives examples of programmed and non-programmed decisions that a manager might be called upon to make. As you go through it, see if you agree with the classification and whether you could add any examples of your own. Remember that what may be a programmed decision to you may be a non-programmed decision to someone else who is unfamiliar with the situation.

Checklist 3.1 Decisions

- **Situations that usually require mainly programmed decisions**

    processing a repeat order

    calling a team meeting

    allocating work

    appraising a member of your staff

    preparing a monthly report

    determining an employee's sickness benefit

- **Situations that usually require mainly non-programmed decisions**

    launching a new product or service

    taking over another company

    taking on new staff

    changing working practices

    making staff redundant

    moving to new offices

Simon (1960) has long been interested in using computers to simplify some of the stages in making non-programmed decisions. As a result, he has developed a three-stage 'rational' model of decision making. The three stages of Simon's model are:

- intelligence – analysing the problem that requires a decision
- design – considering and inventing possible courses of action
- choice – selecting the best course of action

Let's take as an example of a non-programmed decision the buying of a car. Your present car requires a considerable amount of money spent on it to make it roadworthy (intelligence stage). What options might be open to you? You might:

- buy a new car
- buy a second-hand car

- pay the money required to repair your present car
- give up having a car at all and use public transport

However, there are also other issues that you would have to consider, such as:

- whether you had enough money to repair the present car
- whether you had enough money to buy a new or second-hand car
- the needs of other car-users in your family
- the availability of alternative transport

Then, having made a decision – let's say to buy a second-hand car – there are other decisions to make. Should you buy it:

- now or in a few weeks or months?
- from a second-hand car dealer?
- at a car auction?
- from a private seller?

Eventually, you may make the final decision to buy your second-hand car within the next few weeks from a second-hand car dealer, leaving you still with a set of options as to which dealer to buy from and what kind of car to buy ...

So, as indicated in the foregoing example, Simon's model is an iterative one, requiring the use of the three stages – intelligence, design and choice – more than once in coming to a final decision.

Simon also argued that many decisions, especially those made in the business context, are based on the 'satisficing' approach. That is, a decision is made that will yield a 'good enough' outcome – one that is satisfactory and sufficient in the circumstances – rather than a perfect outcome. The reason for this is that managers and others in organisations are seldom in possession of all the relevant information, nor do they have time to collect and process such information before making the decision. A further reason for the prevalence of 'satisficing' is that it is often a low-risk strategy.

Let us return to the decision involving the car you looked at earlier. Often there just isn't enough time, nor necessarily inclination, to go into all the multiple choices that apply to different models of cars from different years. You may have a few major criteria on which you base your final choice, such as price, age, size (of both car and engine) and reliability; other factors such as accessories, colour, safety, number of doors, sun roof, mileage and so on may be secondary considerations. In other words, you have made a 'satisficing' decision that meets a minimal number of criteria.

In Chapter 1, we looked at a model of management or leadership style that was based on how managers made decisions, ranging from the autocratic manager ('I make all the decisions around here') to the very participative ('Let's all take responsibility for what is decided'). As with leadership, a manager's style of decision making will be dependent not only on whether the decision is a programmed or non-programmed one but also on timescales, organisational expectations and the people involved. Telling everyone to evacuate the building because it is on fire is at the autocratic end of the decision-making scale – but it is hardly the time to be consulting with your colleagues and subordinates about whether or not to evacuate, which exits to use and who should leave first!

Victor Vroom, a Professor at Yale University, has also studied decision making by managers through giving them a set of problem descriptions and asking them for their preferred solutions. He found that individual managers used a wide range of processes when coming to a decision. No managers indicated that they would use the same process for all the decisions they had to reach (Pugh and Hickson, 1997). Vroom created a complex decision model based on seven questions that he suggested managers should apply to any possible decision:

(1) Is there a quality requirement which would make one solution more rational than another?
(2) Do I have sufficient information to make a high-quality decision?
(3) Is this problem structured?
(4) Is acceptance of the decision by subordinates critical to effective implementation?
(5) If I made the decision on my own, would it be accepted by my subordinates?

(6) Do subordinates share the organisation's goals, which would be achieved by solving this problem?
(7) Is conflict among subordinates likely in the preferred solution?

Depending on whether you answer 'Yes' or 'No' to each of these questions, a decision tree can be built up which – supposedly – will lead you to the optimum decision. The process is too complex for inclusion here but can be found in Vroom and Yetton's 1973 book, *Leadership and Decision Making*.

Another set of questions that you might apply to any decision is given in Checklist 3.2.

Checklist 3.2   **Questions to ask of any decision**

Have I got all the information I need to make the decision?
If I don't have all the information:

- do I need more

- where can I get it?

Will it actually work?
How costly is it likely to be in terms of:

- money

- human resources

- other resources (plant, equipment etc.)?

Who will be involved in implementing the decision?
Will they actually implement the decision?
Who will be affected by the decision?
Will they accept the decision or resist it?
If they are likely to resist the decision, what can I do to minimise resistance?

➡ **MINIMISING RESISTANCE**

As I've already pointed out, not all decisions require, nor would benefit from, widespread consultation, particularly in a potentially life-threatening situation. Most programmed decisions don't require consultation and, as a manager, you have both the power and authority to make certain decisions. But, in certain cases, making a decision about other people can cause resistance, anxiety and unrest if those affected are not consulted.

Example 1

Let's take as an example a small company that has grown considerably over the past two years. The organisation chart – an 'organigram' – is given in Figure 3.1.

As you can see from the organigram, the company now employs 68 staff and there is good reason to believe that it will continue to expand. It is currently housed in a building designed to accommodate 50 people and there have been increasing complaints of overcrowding. The company has managed to acquire another building close by that will accommodate up to 30 people, and planning permission has already been granted to change its use, if necessary, into production premises as well as offices. The Marketing Director has been given the job of deciding who will move into the new premises and who will stay where they are.

Imagine you have the task given to the Marketing Director. Spend a few minutes studying the organigram and see if you could make a quick decision about who should move and who should not.

Having made your decision, here are some facts that you should know about:

- None of the Directors is willing to share an office with anyone else.
- There is no covered walkway between the buildings, which are about 100 metres apart.
- Secretaries refuse to move between the two buildings.
- Despite being 'on the road' for much of the time, both sales teams demand designated office space.
- Directors and Managers insist that they must have their secretaries in offices next door to their own.
- The production teams cannot be split up.
- Marketing and Sales staff demand that they are both situated in the same building.
- The Finance Director insists she is in the same building as the Managing Director and the two Production Directors.

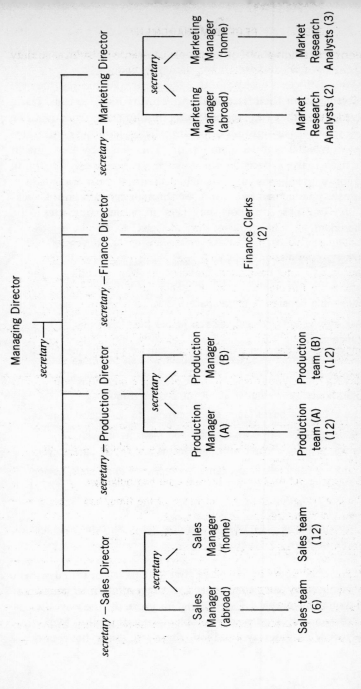

Figure 3.1 Organisation Chart for Buytheway Products

Look back at the first decision you made. Would it satisfy all these demands? And are all the demands realistic?

Moving offices is a very emotive experience. People become very protective about their 'territory' and are very likely to resist being moved unless they can see something in it for them. This might be more space, better lighting or heating, better working conditions, more congenial company and so on. This company has time in which to make a decision that, while not necessarily satisfying everyone, should be one in which natural resistance to the proposed change can be minimised through consultation. Checklist 3.3 outlines some of the ways in which this might be undertaken.

Checklist 3.3 Consulting to minimise resistance

- Call a meeting of all the staff and explain the position.
- Stress the benefits of more space.
- Ask anyone to come and see you if they have particular concerns.
- Ask for constructive suggestions about who should move and who should stay.
- Start a weekly newsletter about the proposed moves.
- Use a bulletin board (actual or electronic) to post developments.
- Hold meetings with each Director and Manager individually, asking them to consult with their teams and report back to you.
- Communicate preliminary, tentative decisions to all staff, asking for comments.
- Ensure you listen to all comments and suggestions.
- Ensure everyone is aware that you have taken all comments and suggestions into account.

Then, once you have ensured that you have consulted widely and taken everyone's comments and suggestions into consideration, you can you make a 'satisficing' decision. (By the way, there is no 'correct' answer to the problem besetting the Marketing Director of Buytheway Products since we don't have enough information and only through consultation will he discover any reasons why people are resisting the move.)

➡ THE PLANNING PROCESS

Planning involves making decisions and, often, making decisions involves planning. Take the example of Buytheway Products; the Marketing Director would probably be involved in planning the move once the overall decision had been made. The kinds of factors he would have to take into account might include:

- the timing of the move – both the date and duration
- structural changes to be made in both buildings to accommodate change in use
- siting of computer trunking, and telephone and electrical points
- packing and unpacking of personal, office and/or production equipment
- removal of personal/office/production equipment
- technical assistance in setting up computing and other equipment

Like decison making, some kinds of planning are easier than others. The more complex the project and the more people involved in it, the more care needs to be taken in planning at every stage. And you have to recognise that what seems to you and others as a near-perfect plan can collapse if there is an unforeseen crisis: no plan is ever perfect.

Checklist 3.4 gives an eight-stage process for planning. The stages are outlined in more detail below but as you read through the checklist, think about the plan the Marketing Director of Buytheway has to construct for the relocation of staff.

Checklist 3.4   The eight-stage planning process

Stage 1 Define the objectives.

Stage 2 Generate and evaluate the options.

Stage 3 Identify the activities.

Stage 4 Sequence the activities.

Stage 5 Identify the resources.

Stage 6 Review the plan.

Stage 7 Prepare action plans and schedules.

Stage 8 Monitor and control; replan if necessary.

(*The Effective Manager*, 1996)

Stage 1: Define the objectives

This stage involves determining exactly what outcome(s) you want to achieve. In the case of Buytheway, the objectives would be something like:

- to relocate staff as agreed with the minimum of disturbance and within a specified timescale
- to ensure production and sales are not disrupted unduly during the move

It is worth spending time on defining your objectives whenever you start the planning process so that you, and others involved, are clear about *what* you want to achieve. *How* you will achieve these objectives is considered in Stages 2–5.

Stage 2: Generate and evaluate the options

This stage is concerned with the different courses of action you might take to achieve your objectives. This is another point at which you should think about involving and consulting other people as to different ways in which you might meet your stated objectives. For example, the Marketing Director might consider moving everyone at once – a 'big bang' approach – or instead making a series of smaller moves over a longer timescale. He might think about moving equipment first, then people, or the other way around, and so on.

When it comes to choosing the best option, factors such as the timescale and cost will usually affect your decision, as well as individual and group preferences. You might favour the 'big bang' approach, getting everything over and done with as quickly as possible. But what if one of the production teams was in the midst of producing a large and important order during that time? Moving them would create delays and customer dissatisfaction, thus defeating one of the objectives.

Stage 3: Identify the activities

Having chosen your best option, you move to Stage 3 to identify the activities. At last you feel you are reaching some real planning! Stage 3 involves identifying all the different activities that would need to be carried out if your best option is going to be successful. At this stage, all you need is a list – not in any order, but one that covers all the different activities related to the move. Some of these activities were identified in a general way in the first paragraph of this section, but a fuller list might look something like this:

- Ensure everyone knows the timings and dates of the relocation and when they will be expected to move.
- Have someone draw up floor plans so everyone knows where they are moving to.
- Get quotations from a removal company.
- Order packing cases.
- Organise redecoration of new building.
- Order new floor coverings.
- Order new office furniture.
- Arrange delivery of furniture.
- Check on structural alterations (e.g. partition walls, computer trunking) needed in both buildings.
- Check that the end result of all alterations meets Health and Safety regulations.
- Book technical assistance for setting up the computers and their network.
- Contact the telephone company about new lines and handsets.
- Let customers and staff know new telephone numbers.

- Check to see whether any production equipment needs to be replaced.
- Delegate relevant tasks.
- Organise a buffet lunch for everyone on moving day.

This list is not necessarily complete and you should go over it several times, adding any further activities as they come to mind. A good idea is to check your list with someone else – you're bound to have forgotten something!

Stage 4: Sequence activities

This is where you put the activities into some sort of priority ordering. For example, you can't have new furniture delivered until the new floor coverings are in place and, obviously, any redecoration would have to take place after structural alterations had been made. There are techniques for helping you to sequence activities, and these techniques will be described briefly later in this chapter. In the meantime, have a try at sequencing the activities given for the relocation of the staff at Buytheways.

Stage 5: Identify the resources

This is the time to consider the resources – financial, human, material, time, power, equipment, information and so on – that you will need in order to carry out your list of activities. It may be, at this point, that you discover you do not have all the resources you need. The Finance Director may have put a ceiling on the amount to be spent on the relocation, or the people to whom you had hoped to delegate some of the tasks will not be available at that time. Whether or not you have all the resources you need, the next stage is to review your plan.

Stage 6: Review the plan

'Review' here means going over the plan again *in detail*. Have you included all the activities? Is your sequencing the best way of carrying out your plan? If you don't have adequate resources, what can you do about this? You may need to alter your plan in the light of resource availability or make a case for any extra resources you need. And you need to go back and look at your objectives. Perhaps they need to be revised – they may be too ambitious or just not feasible within the time available and with less resources than you had hoped. Reviewing the plan may, in fact, mean starting all over again.

Stage 7: Prepare action plans and schedules

However, let's assume the plan has been reviewed and is not showing any major flaws so that you can move on to Stage 7. The action plans and schedules to be prepared are detailed sets of instructions as to who is to do what and how, and when tasks need to be carried out. These visible plans and schedules are for your benefit as much as for those who will be following them. It is your way of keeping a check on progress and co-ordinating what can be a considerable number of activities being carried out by other people.

Stage 8: Monitor and control; replan if necessary

The eighth and final stage is essential: monitor and control; replan if necessary. It's no good handing out the schedules and expecting people to get on with things. Something is bound to go wrong: someone falls behind schedule or goes off sick; equipment fails; the office furniture company goes out of business; the computer technician breaks a leg; the structural alterations fail to meet the Health and Safety regulations; one of the schedules is impossible to maintain. As a manager, it is your job to keep a check on what is going on (monitoring) and make adjustments to the plans and schedules when necessary (control).

➡ PLANNING TECHNIQUES

So far, we have described one very simple planning technique – the list. In its limited way, making a list is a good start in the planning process. You can list the options for achieving the task, list the activities that need to be undertaken, and reorder this list into one that prioritises the activities and allocates times to them. However, there are a number of other relatively simple planning techniques that are useful for different stages in the planning process.

The evaluation matrix

Stage 2 in the planning process involves generating and *evaluating* options. You could use a simple table that sets out all the options in one column and lists all the advantages and disadvantages in two further columns. An evaluation matrix is rather like this but it gives a weighting to each factor.

The evaluation matrix in Figure 3.2 is based on the options suggested earlier concerning the relocation of staff at Buytheways. For each option there are, on the diagonals, the factors that can be weighted. We can see that moving different parts of the company at different times is likely to incur higher costs, take more time and

✓ = low/short ✓✓ = medium ✓✓✓ = high	Financial costs	Disruption	Timescale	Customer inconvenience
Move everyone at the same time	✓✓	✓✓	✓	✓
Move Production first, then Sales, then Marketing, then Directorate	✓✓✓	✓	✓✓✓	✓✓
Move equipment then people	✓✓	✓✓✓	✓✓	✓✓
Move people then equipment	✓✓	✓✓✓	✓✓	✓✓

Figure 3.2 The evaluation matrix

cause more inconvenience to customers than moving everyone at once. In fact, all options appear to incur heavier weightings than the first one. Although this is a rough-and-ready technique in relation to a complex project such as this one, it can highlight the 'best' option or show which one(s) should be discounted altogether. In fact, it is not only a planning technique but also an aid to decision making. An evaluation matrix would be very helpful, for example, in deciding between different models of second-hand cars.

The Gantt chart

A Gantt chart is particularly useful for planning a sequence of activities over a given timescale. It is also useful because it is a simple and effective way of showing other people what has to be done in a certain period. There is an example of a Gantt chart in Figure 3.3.

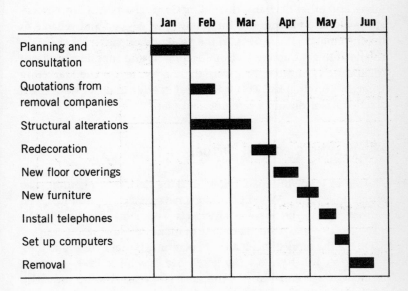

Figure 3.3 The Gantt chart

The chart is a fairly simplistic representation of what needs to be done, in what order and during what period of time, but it nevertheless immediately communicates some essential information. People can see why the move cannot take place until late May or early June, for example, because of the refurbishment of the new building. It is readily understandable and, like many diagrammatic representations, is 'worth a thousand words'.

A flowchart

A flowchart, beloved of engineers, is another diagrammatic method of showing a sequence of activities although, unlike the Gantt chart, it usually doesn't indicate timescales, merely the order in which activities will be undertaken. However, as the flowchart in Figure 3.4 demonstrates, it can be used to present other kinds of information, such as who will be responsible for tasks.

There are computer software packages designed to assist with the planning process that can produce impressive-looking charts, tables and other diagrams (including Gantt charts and flowcharts). However, any planning technique is only as good and reliable as the information it contains. In the flowchart opposite, for example, the need to get quotations from decorators and suppliers has been (deliberately) omitted. Nor were these activities on the Marketing Director's original list. This is the kind of error that can slow down a schedule or distort a carefully laid plan.

➡ PLANNING FOR THE FUTURE

As well as involving managers in making decisions, planning also entails forecasting. When planning a new project, for example, you cannot expect to be certain of all aspects of it; there will be times when you have to make estimates of time or money or other resources.

One of the more difficult areas of planning is that of future staffing levels. You will have a fairly good idea of who is likely to reach retirement age and leave in the next few years, but no idea who might leave through ill-health, a change in personal circumstances or for a better job. You can, however, make an estimate, using staff

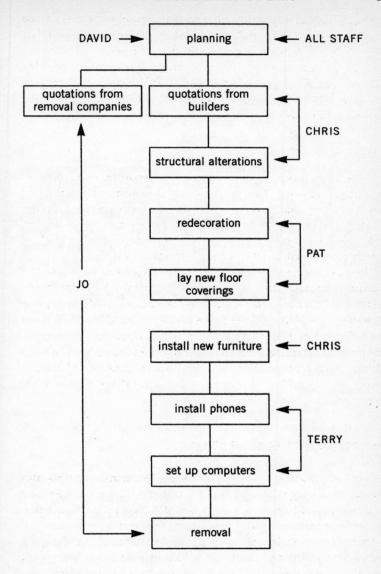

Figure 3.4 A flowchart

turnover from past years to give you an average yearly turnover. The equation for measuring turnover as a percentage is as follows:

$$\frac{\text{Number of people leaving your area of responsibility in one year}}{\text{Average number of people in your area of responsibility during same period}} \times 100$$

Thus, if your department had an average number of 120 employees last year, of whom 30 left, you had a staff turnover of 25% for that year. Over a number of years, you can calculate an average staff turnover as a guide to succession and staff planning. However, you also need to analyse the turnover statistics in terms of what categories of people left and why. Checklist 3.5 suggests a number of issues you need to consider when looking at turnover statistics.

Checklist 3.5   Questions to ask about turnover statistics

- Is there a pattern – for example, is turnover higher for some grades of staff than for others?
- How many staff left at retirement age?
- How many staff left before retirement age?
- How many staff left within 1, 2 or 5 years of service with the organisation?
- What is the average length of service of those who left before retirement age?
- Was there any planned redundancy during the period you are looking at?
- Was there any other factor, such as relocation or changes in working practices during the period you are looking at?

This kind of analysis can build up quite a sophisticated portrait of staff turnover, allowing you to forecast your staffing needs for the next few years at least – that is, unless there is a change in the organisation's fortunes, one way or another, or it is taken over by, or merged with, another company. It helps you to consider succession planning: who is eligible for promotion, who needs more training, what skills are missing and may need to be bought in.

It will also be an opportunity for you to look at *why* people leave. Checklist 3.6 below lists some reasons why people leave.

Checklist 3.6   Reasons why people leave

- offered another job with better pay and/or working conditions
- personal circumstances change – e.g. partner gets a job in another part of the country
- planned move to part-time work or flexi-working
- low commitment to the organisation
- don't value rewards offered
- poor working conditions
- low pay
- low status
- no opportunities for promotion/advancement
- lack of training and development opportunities
- ill-health
- too much travelling
- anti-social hours
- over-zealous supervision
- interpersonal or inter-group conflict

Many of these reasons are internal to the organisation. As well as the causes of low morale and commitment that we shall be looking at in the next chapter, you need to consider your organisation's recruitment and selection practices. Are you recruiting the right people for the right jobs? Are you providing sufficient induction, training and development opportunities for staff? Are you employing highly skilled people in routine, repetitious jobs?

➡ CHRIS'S PROBLEM (3)

Once again, Chris has come to you with a problem. 'They've put me in charge of staff training and development. I'm supposed to come up with a menu of courses and training opportunities for all six departments and organise who goes on them, who runs them and so on. I suppose that means I'll need to talk to all the Heads of Department and tell them what I'm doing. I really don't know where to start – how do I find out about what courses are available, for example? Then I'll need to plan when they are going to run, I suppose, and you know what it's like when you plan anything around here. Nobody agrees with what you've done, everyone just goes off and does their own thing and everything falls apart.'

Based on what you have read, how would you advise Chris to set about planning for staff training and development?

References

Pugh D. S. and Hickson D. J., *Writers on Organisations* 5th edn (Penguin, London, 1997)

Simon H. A., *The New Science of Management Decision* (Harper Row, London, 1960)

The Effective Manager (Open University Business School, Milton Keynes, 1996)

Vroom V. H. and Yetton P. W., *Leadership and Decision-Making* (University of Pittsburgh Press, Pittsburgh US, 1973)

Chapter 4
Job satisfaction, rewards and commitment

'As a general view, remuneration by fixed salaries does not in any class of functionaries produce the maximum amount of zeal.'

(John Stuart Mill, 1849)

John Stuart Mill was writing 150 years ago and what he said then was considered to be quite controversial. He also wrote in the same book, *Principles of Political Economy*, that 'The efficiency of industry may be expected to be great, in proportion as the fruits of industry are insured to the person exerting it.' In other words – for Mill was a trifle long-winded – money alone, particularly if it is a fixed salary, does not motivate people to work harder, but if a person values the rewards and outcomes of the work, then he or she will perform well. Do you agree with these statements?

The subject matter of this chapter is concerned with motivation, job satisfaction, rewards and employee commitment. We looked at some of the reasons why people leave organisations at the end of the last chapter. Here, we look at why they stay.

➡ SOME DEFINITIONS

Words such as 'motivation', 'satisfaction' and 'commitment' are often used as if these states are interchangeable, but there are subtle differences.

Motivation

'A well motivated person is someone with clearly defined goals who takes action which he or she expects will achieve these goals' (Armstrong, 1992). You will be looking at some of the goals people want to achieve in this chapter, including rewards and valued outcomes, and some of the theories about motivation. Motivation can be either extrinsic – that is, externally driven through such factors as reward structures, threats of punishment, pay or promotion – or intrinsic – feelings of achievement, a job well done, pleasure in the end product.

Satisfaction

There are two uses of the word 'satisfaction' in the work context. The first of these refers to satisfaction of needs and is closely related to motivational factors. The second use of the word is in the phrase 'job satisfaction'. This latter use includes the satisfaction of needs but also other contributory factors such as good working conditions, the company of others, the pleasure of seeing a task completed. High job satisfaction does not necessarily mean high performance; low job satisfaction, on the other hand, can be strongly related to staff turnover.

Outcomes

Outcomes are the results of work and valued outcomes can increase performance. Outcomes may include tangible rewards (see next subsection) but could also be intangibles such as pride in doing a good job, seeing a task through to the end, or receiving praise. Outcomes may also be negative – receiving criticism, being blamed for poor work, being denied the opportunity to work overtime.

Rewards

Like outcomes, rewards are not always tangible. Tangible rewards are usually financial (wages/salary, bonuses etc.) but can also come in the form of 'perks' such as a company car, healthcare, a holiday and so on.

Commitment

Commitment – to the job, to the organisation – is a more stable and long-lasting condition than either motivation or satisfaction. It has been defined as follows:

- a belief in, and acceptance of, the organisation itself and/or its goals and values
- a willingness to exert effort on behalf of the organisation beyond what is contracted for, which might include giving private time to work, postponing a holiday, or making some other personal sacrifice for the organisation without the expectation of immediate personal gain
- a desire to maintain membership of the organisation

(White, 1987)

You would expect organisations to try to engender commitment in their employees, and many do. Particularly high levels of commitment are to be found in voluntary and non-profit enterprises, for example, since those that work for such organisations usually share their beliefs and values.

➡ HOW PEOPLE BEHAVE AT WORK

Look at some examples of people at work.

Example 1

Jack was always on time for work and never left before it was time to go home. He was keen and enthusiastic about everything he did and full of new ideas. If someone was off sick or on holiday, he would often take over their work without being asked and would manage to perform both jobs well. He was also very good with new trainees, spending a lot of time with them patiently explaining how the job should be done. Now he is a changed person. He comes in late and leaves early if he can get away with it. He is often off sick, but only for a day or two so that he doesn't require a doctor's note. He has become lazy and slipshod at work and has complained recently that he doesn't have the time to train other people as well as doing his own job.

Example 2

Audrey was quiet and shy, never able to speak up for herself. She was never in line for promotion since she performed the job only adequately. No one thought she could take the added responsibility that promotion would entail anyway. So she worked away quietly at the same job for a number of years. Then her manager retired and a new one took her place. She was a very dynamic, ambitious person and had no time for what she considered to be routine or boring work, which she delegated to Audrey. The manager insisted on checking everything Audrey did, however, which probably took her just as long as doing the work herself. Audrey never complained and the extra work got done. Until, one day, Audrey quietly got up from her desk, put on her coat and left.

Example 3

Everybody knew Dan was very bright. He had a good university degree and was nicknamed 'the Prof' by his work mates. He had tried to get a job where he could use his degree when he left university, but failed to find anything suitable. All he could hope for was to work his way up in the company the hard way. He was likeable, reliable and hardworking but, after two years with the company, he was still doing the same job. His work mates noticed that he was becoming irritable and short-tempered and that his work was becoming erratic. Sometimes he forgot to make an extra turn on a screw or left off a bolt so that the supervisor would have to return what he had been working on. One day he was found drinking a can of beer in his work break, which was strictly against company rules, and he is now facing a disciplinary interview.

What went wrong? We could say that all these employees lost their motivation to work, but why did they do so? Checklist 4.1 lists some factors that can lead to low motivation at work. As you read through the checklist, think about the examples of the employees above and consider which reasons might have led to their changed behaviour. You might also like to think about any of your own staff at work who seem to have lost motivation and reflect on whether any of the reasons given below might be contributory.

Checklist 4.1 **Causes of low motivation at work**

- boring, repetitive work
- low use of skills
- poor working conditions
- work overload
- no recognition for work well done
- lack of feedback on performance
- no opportunities for advancement
- low status
- poor interpersonal relationships
- little or no responsibility for work undertaken
- over-zealous supervision.

In the three examples given above, it is possible that Jack was getting no recogniton for the extra work he was taking on. It is very easy to accept the 'willing workhorse' and forget to give praise or thanks when they are due. In Audrey's case, she was suffering from a combination of work overload and over-zealous supervision. This also meant she was getting very little responsibility for the work she was doing. Finally, Dan's skills were obviously not being used in the routine work he was undertaking. He had hoped for advancement, but this had not happened.

These three cases were fairly obvious and real life is not always as clear-cut. If you thought about any of your staff's reasons for low motivation, they were probably more complex than the examples I gave. You should also think about factors outside work, such as domestic troubles, financial worries or family illness, which could also affect a person at work.

➡ SATISFYING NEEDS

Motivation theories can generally be divided into those that argue that motivation is needs-related and those that consider it to be goal-related.

The best-known needs-related theory of motivation is that of Maslow, who devised a hierarchy of needs as shown in Figure 4.1. He believed that people worked to satisfy needs in a hierarchical order so that once a lower-order need was satisfied, the person would begin to search for ways to satisfy the next need on the ladder.

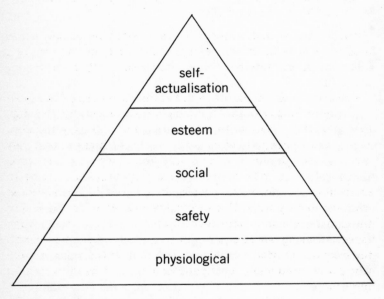

Figure 4.1 Maslow's hierarchy of needs

The lowest order of needs are *physiological* ones – hunger, thirst, warmth. In most cases, people at work have already satisfied these needs through having money to pay for them. Physiological needs are those that the homeless are searching to satisfy.

Maslow explained *safety* needs by referring first to children. Consider the following quotation:

The average child in our society generally prefers a safe, orderly, predictable, organised world, which he can count on, and in which unexpected, unmanageable or other dangerous things do not happen, and in which, in any case, he has all-powerful parents who protect and shield him from harm.

The healthy, normal, fortunate adult in our culture is largely satisfied in his safety needs. The peaceful, smoothly running, 'good' society ordinarily makes its members feel safe enough from wild animals, extremes of temperature, criminals, assault, murder, tyranny etc. Therefore, in a very real sense, he no longer has any safety needs as active motivators. Just as a sated person no longer feels hungry, a safe person no longer feels endangered.' (Maslow, 1943).

Maslow argues that, in today's society, safety needs only act as motivators at times of crisis that threaten safety or life, such as a fire, natural catastrophes, crime waves and other emergency situations.

However, when people move up to satisfy *social* needs, these can act as motivators at work. Most people need to feel they 'belong', that they have a place in the work group and in the organisation. Most people don't go to work just to put in the hours so that they can earn enough money to enjoy the times they are not at work. Congenial work colleagues can be a very important factor in motivation and, for many people, their closest friends are those with whom they work. Unemployed people often cite the loss of the camaraderie and companionship at work as one of the worst aspects of being out of a job. While, in many Western countries, the state will provide a certain amount of financial help for those who cannot find a job, it cannot provide the social interaction of the workplace.

If the work satisfies social needs, the next stage in the hierarchy is that of *esteem* needs. These are needs relating to self-respect or self-esteem and respect for others. To have self-esteem, you need to feel a sense of achievement in what you do and to gain the respect of those you work with. From self-esteem stem feelings of self-confidence and self-worth.

Finally, at the top of the hierarchy, Maslow puts the complex concept of *self-actualisation*, which he describes as 'A musician must make music, an artist must paint, a poet must write if he is to be ultimately happy. What a man *can* be, he *must* be.' (Maslow, 1943) (I apologise for what is now regarded as sexist language in the quotations from Maslow, but he was writing before awareness of gender-free language was raised.)

If you look back to the earlier examples of people behaving oddly at work, you can see how these could fit with needs-related theories of motivation. Both Jack and Audrey could be seen to be seeking self-esteem and not finding it in their work situations. In the case of Dan, it is more likely that he had a strong need for self-actualisation but the routine work he was undertaking was frustrating this need.

➡ JOB SATISFACTION

Professor Frederick Herzberg of the University of Utah has spent many years researching motivation in the work situation and its effects on job satisfaction. After a major study of engineers and accounts, he was able to show (1966) what kinds of events or activities led to job satisfaction or dissatisfaction. Checklist 4.2 outlines the factors that contribute to both states.

| Checklist 4.2 | Determinants of job satisfaction/dissatisfaction |

- achievement
- recognition
- the nature of the work itself
- responsibility
- advancement
- company policy and administration
- supervision
- salary
- interpersonal relationships
- working conditions

According to Herzberg's findings, the first five factors in Checklist

4.2 were the strongest determinants of job satisfaction. However, when asked about factors that contributed to *dis*satisfaction at work, these five factors were mentioned very infrequently. Dissatisfaction was usually connected with company policy and administration, supervision, salary, interpersonal relations and working conditions. Instead of job satisfaction and job dissatisfaction being the opposite of each other, Herzberg concluded that they were concerned with two different ranges of human needs. The factors associated with job satisfaction, Herzberg saw as being related to self-actualisation needs, while those associated with job dissatisfaction were related to the need to avoid physical and social deprivation (Pugh and Hickson, 1997).

In his theory of motivation, Herzberg stresses the practical nature of his research. To increase motivation, managers and employers need to ensure that the factors contributing to job satisfaction are present. As far as the factors affecting job dissatisfaction are concerned, removing them or improving them will reduce job dissatisfaction – but it will not increase motivation.

In order to increase motivation through increased job satisfaction, Herzberg suggested that 'job enrichment' should be the manager's aim. Checklist 4.3 outlines the principles of job enrichment according to Herzberg. As you read through it, ask yourself if there are any ways in which you might enrich the jobs of the people for whom you are responsible, or how your own job might be enriched.

Checklist 4.3   The principles of job enrichment

- Remove some controls while retaining accountability.
- Increase the responsibility of individuals for their own work.
- Give individuals complete, natural units of work.
- Give additional authority to an employee.
- Make reports directly available to the individual rather than through a supervisor.
- Introduce new and more challenging tasks not previously undertaken.
- Assign specific or specialised tasks to individuals, enabling them
  to become experts.

A more recent survey of factors that affect job satisfaction is given in Checklist 4.4. People in work were asked to rate the various aspects of their jobs that contributed to their individual job satisfaction. Again, think about your own job and whether you agree with the ratings given in the checklist as you read it.

Checklist 4.4 **Factors in job satisfaction**

Factor	Rating %
The respect of the people you work with	88
Personal freedom	87
Learning something new	86
Helping other people	84
A challenge	83
Being asked for advice	82
Respect of people in your field	78
Being well trained	76
Being liked by the people you work with	74
Influencing events	74
Working conditions	71
Being offered increasing responsibility	69
Completing a project	68
Being part of a team	65
Meeting people through work	65
Influencing people	64
Working as an individual	63
Starting a project	61
Solving a human relations problem	59
Security	55
Being praised by superiors	53
Status in the organisation	50
Being promoted	45
Solving a technical problem	45

Setting up a new system	43
Status of your organisation	42
Making money	40
Exercising power	26
Social status	19

(Knight, 1989)

As you can see from Checklist 4.4, there are many similarities with Herzberg's determinants of job satisfaction. Money comes very low in the ratings, but we shall be looking at pay and financial rewards later in this chapter.

➡ GOAL-RELATED MOTIVATION

A third set of ideas about motivation are those related to goal-setting and achievement. If we accept that recognition for a job well done, achievement and the nature of the work itself all contribute to job satisfaction, then unless goals are set, individuals will never know whether or not they have achieved them.

Latham and Locke (1979) are the strongest proponents of goal setting as a motivational technique. They conducted an experiment for the American Pulpwood Association, which had become concerned about increasing the productivity of independent loggers. These loggers were self-employed entrepreneurs and free to work however many days a week they wanted. Most of them worked the absolute minimum. Although there had been advances in technology that would make the industry less dependent on the loggers, many logging supervisors had only limited finances and could not afford the more advanced equipment. As Latham and Locke stated in their 1979 article, '... we designed a survey that would help managers determine "what makes these people tick".'

They discovered that there were three types of supervisors: one group stayed with the loggers, provided instruction, explanation and training and had little problem with financing operations; another group left the loggers alone during the day, provided little training and set them production goals for the day or week. In neither of these groups was production particularly high. The third group of supervisors stayed with their group, provided training, instruction and explanations and set specific production goals; and the productivity of this group was high.

The experiment was repeated several times and, consistently, the setting of specific production goals combined with on-the-job supervision resulted in improved productivity. When asked why this was the case, the loggers revealed in interviews that:

- a difficult but attainable goal increases the challenge of the job
- a specific goal makes it clear what is expected of you
- goal feedback via record-keeping and observation provides a sense of achievement, recognition and accomplishment

By now, you should be getting some idea of how to motivate people at work through giving them increased responsibility and recognition, a sense of achievement, opportunities for advancement and use of their skills, clear goals, and feedback on how they are performing. But, this is not the whole story....

➡ OUTCOMES

Expectancy theory, as argued by Porter and Lawler (1968) is based on what the individual expects to gain from the amount of effort put into his or her work performance. Again, let's look at two examples.

Example 4

Judy is a consistently high performer. She is keen to get as much training as possible and increase her skills even further. She is in line for promotion next year, although she is younger than most people for the grade to which she aspires. Her manager regards her as highly motivated and only wishes all his staff were of the same calibre.

Example 5

Jorge, however, is his manager's despair. His work is barely adequate but just acceptable enough to ensure he gets by. His manager is certain Jorge has great potential – he is one of those people who see the best in everybody – but he has no idea how to persuade Jorge to improve his performance.

Imagine you were Judy's and Jorge's manager and it was time for their annual appraisal. You would probably look forward to appraising Judy, discussing her next career move, what training and development she wanted and (I hope) giving her due praise for her high performance. Few managers would relish appraising Jorge. It would be difficult to find anything praiseworthy to say to him. Quite possibly, he would be even less motivated to improve his performance after the appraisal interview.

However, if you asked them both what they expected if they worked harder, you would probably get two different answers. Judy, for example, might say that she wanted promotion and knew this was possible if she maintained, or even increased, her present high performance. Promotion, status, increased responsibility were all important outcomes for her. Jorge, on the other hand, couldn't be less interested in promotion, not even for the extra money it would mean. What he wants is a different job – in Sales rather than in Production – but he doesn't see that happening if he improves his performance in the job he already has. He has seen what happens if you do that – you get more work of the same kind, which is the last thing he wants. They both expect different outcomes from putting in extra effort in their jobs.

Do you have any idea about the outcomes your staff expect from the amount of effort they put into the work they are doing? Are the outcomes clearly stated anywhere or explained to them? And even if they are, do they all want or expect the same outcomes? It is highly unlikely. To be effective in motivating people to improve performance, there has to be a clearly understood relationship between performance and outcome, and the outcome has to be seen to be a way of satisfying the individual's needs. Therefore, if you work harder than everyone else all year but, at year-end, everyone receives the same bonus, there is no clear link between performance and outcome and you are likely to feel aggrieved and reconsider your working patterns. You would feel equally aggrieved if, after expecting a bonus, none was forthcoming.

➡ REWARDS

Many outcomes are also rewards – such as the bonus mentioned above. However, there can be a wide range of rewards, as Checklists 4.5 (financial) and 4.6 (indirect and non-financial) demonstrate.

Financial rewards

As you read through Checklist 4.5 on financial rewards, check which ones you and others benefit from in your organisation.

Checklist 4.5   **Financial rewards**

- salary/wage
- bonus
- profit-sharing scheme
- payment by results
- performance-related pay
- pay rise
- honorarium
- overtime pay
- profit-related pay

As you saw earlier, pay can contribute to job satisfaction, but is not considered to be a highly motivational factor unless it is directly related to performance. There have been a number of schemes that have tried to make this direct link, including profit-related pay, payment by results and performance-related pay.

Profit-related pay schemes became popular in the UK after the introduction of tax relief in the 1986 budget. By 1995, over two million employees were covered by the scheme (Clark, 1996). Such a scheme ties the employee's pay to company profits; if the profits go up, so does the employee's salary or wage. This arrangement is similar to performance-related pay, which is more widely used in non-profit-making organisations, where increased or improved performance results in higher pay – and, of course, low performance results in low pay. Similarly, payment by results, although not so widely used, directly links effort to financial reward.

These schemes are based on Porter and Lawler's expectancy theory, namely that if employees see clearly the links between improved performance and outcome (higher pay), then profit-related pay, performance-related pay or payment by results will act as motivators. However, as we have seen, money alone is not usually a motivator; the employee has to value it as a reward for the scheme to work. In a survey of profit-related pay schemes carried out three years after the introduction of tax relief, 67% of those surveyed stated that the scheme made no difference to the amount of effort they put into their work (Poole and Jenkins, 1988).

Indirect and non-financial rewards

Checklist 4.6 is the result of an extensive survey of rewards that are not paid as part of wages or salaries. It is particularly interesting because it shows how different levels of employee regard these rewards – directors, managers, white-collar staff and manual workers. Again, check which of these rewards are available in your organisation and how you rate them compared with the different levels of employee in the checklist.

Checklist 4.6 **Indirect and non-financial rewards**

Reward	All Employees	Directors	Managers	Staff	Manual workers
	%	%	%	%	%
Company sick pay scheme	64	52	55	58	46
Subsidised vending service	51	40	43	45	40
Contributory pension	49	42	49	51	40
Free life insurance	47	41	40	40	30

Uniforms/overalls provided	46	9	13	21	55
Christmas gifts or bonuses	39	23	30	34	30
Sports/social club	30	13	13	13	15
Subsidised canteen	27	12	13	13	13
Additional holidays	26	17	21	21	16
Private health insurance	20	26	21	13	9
Discounted company products	21	14	16	16	15
Private health treatment	15	54	45	24	9
Company car	12	73	67	31	2
Support for education	8	5	11	24	13
Professional subscriptions	8	14	14	8	3
Non-contributory pension	7	26	15	13	9
Study leave	7	1	4	15	6
Flexible working hours	7	9	9	11	6
Home telephone paid/supplied	4	38	26	16	2
Luncheon vouchers/ subsidised meals	4	1	1	1	1
Staff outings	3	2	2	2	2
Car telephone	2	31	15	9	0
Petrol or travel allowance	2	12	10	5	0
Free annual medical check	2	15	6	2	1

Preferential loans/ mortgage	1	1	2	4	2
Season ticket/travel costs	0.5	2	2	2	0

(Bramley and Moon, 1988)

As you can see from the checklist, some rewards – sickness payments, contributory pension schemes, free life insurance and subsidised canteens for example – are fairly evenly spread across all levels of employees. Others, however, appear to be linked to seniority (private health treatment and insurance, company car, telephone, petrol and travel expenses and free annual medical check-ups) and yet others to the job itself (free uniforms/overalls for manual workers).

The (correct) conclusion you have probably reached by now is that there is a range of outcomes and rewards that may or may not act as motivators or contribute to job satisfaction, depending on the individual's circumstances and values. Assessing what these circumstances and values are is an important part of a manager's job, although, sadly, the manager often may not be able to influence the organisation's provision of rewards.

➡ COMMITMENT

Emphasis on employee commitment to the organisation is becoming more tenuous as companies downsize or increase the number of short-term working contracts. School leavers and university graduates no longer expect a career for life in the same organisation. Many older people, who did expect such a career for life and who demonstrated high commitment to the organisations in which they worked, now find themselves unemployed long before they expected.

Martin and Nicholls (1987) suggested three major foundations for creating commitment:

- a sense of belonging to the organisation
- a sense of excitement in the job
- confidence in management

Having a sense of belonging means believing in the organisation, what it stands for, its mission statement, its products or services, its values. It means being proud of the organisation and believing that it contributes to the general well-being of humanity. Take the example of an organisation that is researching into the manufacture of life-saving drugs. Employees of that organisation probably believe that what they are doing is going to be of inestimable benefit to the human race; animal rights activists, however, would not agree that testing prototype drugs on animals can be admissible in the search to prolong or save human life. It is highly improbable, therefore, that anyone with sympathies towards animal rights would ever work for such an organisation, let alone have a sense of commitment to it.

'Belonging to the organisation' is also enhanced if employees feel they are a key part of the organisation, that their ideas and complaints are listened to, that they have a share in making decisions, and that they are consulted about major changes.

'Excitement' in the job is more difficult to clarify and describe. It is the sense of looking forward to going into work because of the job itself (one of Herzberg's determinants of job satisfaction) and because of one's colleagues in the workplace. It is obviously about motivation and job satisfaction and it is also about challenge and opportunities.

The third foundation for creating commitment is that of having confidence in the management of the organisation, in its leadership and in its success. Eventually, even the most committed employee will lose faith in a steadily failing organisation where management does not appear to know what is happening or where the organisation is going.

Checklist 4.7 outlines the components of a commitment strategy. Consider your own commitment to the organisation you work for as you read it through and analyse which components are present and which are absent.

Checklist 4.7   Components of a commitment strategy

- Define and disseminate the mission and values of the organisation.
- Develop shared objectives by ensuring everyone understands the

strategies of the organisation and participates in setting his or her own objectives within the framework of those strategies.

- Get people involved in defining problems and working out solutions in order that they 'own' any changes that emerge from this process.

- Provide transformational leadership from the top, which can inspire people with a vision for the future.

- Use every medium of communication available so as to ensure that messages about the organisation's mission, values and strategies get across.

- Ensure by example and training that the prevailing management style in the organisation encourages involvement and teamwork.

- Develop processes and an organisational climate that encourage people's growth in terms of skill and higher levels of achievement.

- Introduce company-wide profit or gain-sharing plans that encourage people to identify with the organisation.

- Use induction-training programmes to ensure that new employees form a good impression of the company from the outset.

- Use workshops and other types of training to get people together to discuss the issues facing the company and give them the opportunity to contribute their own ideas.

- Take action on good ideas.

  (Armstrong, 1992)

Although you would expect commitment to the organisation to be a very positive aspect in developing motivation in employees, there are also the costs to be considered. It is, for example, easier to engender commitment in organisations that already have a consultative/partcipative decision-making culture, based on team working and feedback on performance than it is in organisations that have traditionally operated in a more autocratic and controlled culture. Walton (1985) suggests the following costs of commitment for such organisations if they want to implement a commitment strategy:

- investment of extra effort by managers;
- development of new skills and relationships;
- coping with higher levels of uncertainty than before;
- resistance to change;
- coping with greater responsibility;
- higher rates of pay; and
- a move to facilitative supervision.

Changing organisational culture is exceptionally difficult and time-consuming. Many of the 'costs' listed above are expensive in terms of time as well as money.

➡ WHAT CAN YOU DO?

After reading through the components of a commitment strategy, you may be wondering how you, as as manager, could have much, if any, influence on how the organisation gains commitment from its employees. Checklist 4.8 attempts to bring together aspects from all the strands discussed in this chapter by suggesting ways in which you, as a manager, can affect your staff's job satisfaction, rewards and sense of commitment. Go through it carefully and think again about ways in which you can improve your staff's performance.

Checklist 4.8 The manager's guide to improving performance

Increasing job satisfaction

- Give due recognition (praise and thanks) for good performance.
- Give your staff increased responsibility and authority for their work.
- Ensure your staff are clear about opportunities for advancement.
- Give direct and timely feeback to individual members of your staff.
- Look at each job and consider how it could be made more challenging.

- Build on and develop individual skills – and make use of them.
- Provide learning and training opportunities.
- Ask experienced staff to pass on their knowledge and experience to others.
- Look at how working conditions might be improved.
- Set clear, achievable objectives for tasks, ensuring all concerned understand them.

Improving rewards

- Where possible, ensure above-average performance is appropriately rewarded.
- Find out what the rewards are that each individual values.
- Find out what rewards your organisation offers – within your powers as a manager you may be able to offer:
  - additional holidays
  - extra time off
  - flexible hours
  - staff outings
- Try to influence your organisation to provide a 'menu' of rewards, including non-financial ones.

Increasing commitment

- Make sure all your staff are aware of the organisation's mission and values.
- When setting individual/team objectives, relate these to organisational objectives.
- Involve staff in defining problems and working out solutions.
- Encourage team working.
- Ensure you have comprehensive induction training programmes (see Chapter 7).
- Use workshops to get people to discuss organisation-wide issues and contribute ideas.
- Start a suggestion box and take action on good ideas, giving due recognition to the originators.

➡ CHRIS'S PROBLEM (4)

Chris has been asked by a senior manager to look at the performance of specific members of staff in the Department and see what can be done about it. These are habitual under-performers. One is two years away from retirement and is doing the bare minimum; another complains that the work she is doing is boring. Dave seems to have problems getting on with others in the team and Carrie resents having work delegated to her. Alex doesn't appear to want more responsibility because she says she then has to take the blame when things go wrong. There doesn't seem to be any clear reason why Bob performs badly. Finally, three of the clerical staff have formally complained that the office they work in is small and stuffy with inadequate light and ventilation.

What could Chris do to improve the performance of these members of staff?

References

Armstrong M., *A Handbook of Personnel Management Practice*, 4th edn, (Kogan Page, London, 1992)

Bramley J. E. and Moon P., 'New Wage/Salary Benefits', *PPC Group Survey Report* (1988)

Clark G., 'Profit-related Pay: a Retrospective' in *The Effective Manager; Perspectives and Illustrations*, ed. J. Billsberry (Sage, London, 1996)

Herzberg F., *Work and the Nature of Man* (World Publishing Co. 1966)

Knight G. P., 'Why work?' in the *Guardian*, 1989

Latham G. P. and Locke E. A., 'Goal setting: A motivational technique that works' in *Organisational Dynamics* (1979), Vol 8(2), pp. 68–80

Martin P. and Nicholls J., *Creating a Committed Workforce* (Institute of Personnel Management, London, 1987)

Maslow A. H., 'A theory of human motivation', in *Psychological Review* (1943) Vol 50, pp. 370–96

Mill J. S., *Principles of Political Economy* (1848) Book 11, Chapters 1 and 3

Poole M. and Jenkins G., 'How employees respond to profit sharing', *Personnel Management*, July 1988

Porter L. W. and Lawler E. E. III, *Managerial Attitudes and Performance*, (Irwin-Dorsey, Homewood Ill, 1968)

Pugh D. S. and Hickson D. J., *Writers on Organisations*, 5th edn (Penguin, London, 1997)

Walton R. E., 'From Control to Commitment in the Workplace' in *Harvard Business Review* (1985) Vol 63(2), pp. 77–84

White G., *Employee Commitment*, ACAS Work Research Unit Occasional Paper 38, October (ACAS, London, 1987)

Chapter 5
Managing performance and careers

'Managing is the art of getting things done through and with people in formally organised groups. It is the art of creating an environment in which people can perform as individuals and yet co-operate towards attainment of group goals. It is the art of removing blocks to such performance.'

(Koontz, 1962)

Performance measurement and management are two of the cornerstones of managerial effectiveness. Yet, too often, only cursory attention is paid to either activity. If there is no accurate way of measuring performance, how can rewards be allocated equitably? And, if performance is not measured in some way, how can it be managed through performance reviews and appraisal systems, for example?

Performance management needs to be linked to career management, particularly through the appraisal process. In the past, organisations took rather more responsibility for the career moves of their employees than is the case now. Today, with so much uncertainty around concerning the next job and the loss of the concept of 'careers for life' within one organisation, individuals are sharing that responsibility. Performance management, therefore, includes a number of related activities, the most significant of which are depicted in Figure 5.1.

The starting point is an agreed set of objectives with whoever is carrying out the task. As Koontz (1962) says, there is an art here in harmonising individual and group goals and there is a need for the individual and the group to feel they 'own' the objectives that have been set. There is no point in setting objectives which are too

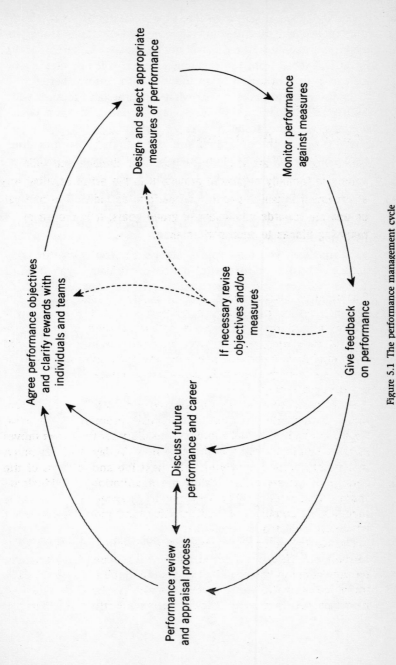

Figure 5.1 The performance management cycle

high or too low: if objectives are too high, they will never be achieved, leaving you and your staff frustrated and demotivated; if objectives are too low, the task will not be seen as challenging and, as you will recall from the previous chapter, will not create job satisfaction or motivation in an individual to perform better.

You also need to make it clear what outcomes and rewards will result from adequate and above-average performance, and what sanctions will apply to below-average performance.

Having agreed the objectives and clarified the outcomes, the next stage is to find some appropriate ways of measuring performance. The important word here is 'appropriate'. Measuring performance is not an easy task, as we shall see below, but whatever measures you choose, they need to be ones that indicate to you and to the individual or group when performance is up to standard and when it is falling below.

As a manager, you (and your supervisors if you work through them) need to monitor performance continually against the selected measures and be prepared to give frequent feedback to those concerned. Sometimes it may be that the measures are inappropriate; sometimes that the objectives are too ambitious. In either case, you would need to review the objectives or the measures. Or, of course, it may be that the people concerned are underperforming, in which case you may need to look at some of the factors we discussed in the last chapter.

The performance review and appraisal processes should be designed to provide feedback on performance and allow the individual to give you feedback on why performance is at the level it is. Appraisal is also the opportunity to discuss future performance, careers and the next set of performance objectives.

➡ OBJECTIVES AND MEASURES OF PERFORMANCE

Researchers into links between setting objectives and motivation have agreed that objectives should be:

- specific
- demanding

- attainable
- accepted by all as desirable
- the subject of feedback
  (Mento et al., 1987)

Objectives should never be vague or woolly, and they need to be clearly understood by everyone who is involved in attaining them. This is why agreement is so important, since it is an opportunity for everyone concerned to question and contribute to a clearly understood and realistic set of objectives.

Designing and selecting performance measures is the next step, and these need to be clearly related to the tasks and the objectives.

Humble (1987) suggests four aspects of performance that managers should look at when designing and selecting measures:

- quantity (how much?)
- quality (how well?)
- time (by when?)
- cost (at what cost?)

Mabey and Salaman (1995) have defined an effective measure of performance to be:

- free from influence from outside factors that are not relevant to the performance of the task
- unable to be manipulated by those performing or monitoring the task
- straightforward and easy to understand
- inexpensive to collect
- relevant to the aspect of performance that is being measured

Checklist 5.1 overleaf gives some suggested performance measures for the recruitment process and then some more general measures that might be applied to other activities. As you read through these, consider whether they meet the criteria for performance measures given above.

Checklist 5.1 | Performance measures

Recruiting new staff

- length of time taken between job becoming vacant and filling the post
- cost of advertising
- cost of recruitment
- ratio of the number of applications from candidates who could perform the job to the number of applications from those who could not
- cost of induction training
- length of time new recruits stay with organisation

Other performance measures

- training and development targets (number of events, numbers attending etc.)
- wastage as a percentage of production
- number of errors in specific time period
- absenteeism
- sales targets
- number of complaints from customers/clients
- time of response to complaints
- delivery times
- staff costs as a percentage of total expenditure
- material costs
- production outputs
- number of mistakes on payroll

All of the above are relatively objective measures since they involve numbers. However, it is not always possible to be entirely objective, particularly when it comes to assessing performance. When it comes to giving feedback on performance or allocating rewards, you may have to cope with a rating scale where individuals are graded in ways such as:

1 outstanding performance – consistent output of high-quality work

2 satisfactory performance – satisfactory level of output and average effort

3 fair – less-than-average output and quality

4 unsatisfactory – poor quality and low output

If the performance measures you selected are relevant and appropriate, they will help you to make a decision along such a scale. But what do you do in the case of the person who produces a low output ('unsatisfactory') of consistently high quality? Or the member of staff whose output is phenomenally high but whose work is of poor quality?

Some of the clearest examples of performance criteria are those produced by the Management Charter Initiative (MCI) in relation to their Management Standards. These standards are the basis for managerial and supervisory performance and are subject to assessment if the individual wants to gain a National Vocational Qualification (NVQ). The assessment is based on evidence from work activities, products and outcomes, written or spoken reports and witness testimony. Below are some MCI suggestions for performance criteria for use in the business environment.

For minimising interpersonal conflict, you should ensure that:

- you inform individuals of the standards of work and behaviour that you expect in a manner, and at a level and pace appropriate to the individuals concerned

- you provide opportunities for individuals to discuss problems that directly or indirectly affect their work

- you take action promptly to deal with conflicts between individuals

- you inform relevant people about conflict outside your area of responsibility

- the way you resolve conflict minimises disruption to work and discord between individuals

- the way you resolve conflict complies with organisational and legal requirements

- your records of conflicts and their outcomes are accurate, and comply with requirements for confidentiality and other organisational policies

- you make recommendations for improving procedures and reducing the potential for conflict to the relevant people

These criteria don't contain numerical measures. MCI suggests a number of ways in which you could gather or provide evidence of meeting these criteria, including:

- keeping minutes or notes of relevant meetings and discussions
- keeping records of relevant correspondence between individuals
- keeping a log or a diary which records your attempt to deal with conflict
- recording conflicts and their outcomes
- taking statements from individuals involved in conflicts
- taking statements from people who observed you resolving conflicts
- giving written or verbal reports on how you gave individuals opportunities to discuss problems directly or indirectly related to their work, how you identified conflicts, and how you decided what action to take to minimise conflict and disruption

You can see from this list that it is possible to design criteria and measures that are not numerically guided but that enable you to gauge how well or how poorly an individual is performing.

➡ THE PERFORMANCE REVIEW

Performance reviews and appraisal systems

In some organisations, 'performance review' and 'appraisal' are the same process. In this chapter, I prefer to use the term 'performance review' as an activity that is ongoing and that serves to provide feedback on a more frequent basis than appraisal. Performance reviews may be carried out by a manager or a direct supervisor, whereas appraisal should normally be carried out by the relevant manager alone. They are necessary because no performance management system can ever be perfect; crises or unplanned events are only too likely to arise and disrupt the smooth pattern of performance. For example, a key worker may leave or be absent through illness; equipment may fail; suppliers might go out of business; customers may change their demands.

Some performance reviews may be relatively informal but need to be formalised to the extent that they:

- occur at regular and frequent intervals, e.g. monthly;
- are directly related to the performance of the task being undertaken;
- are based on performance measures;
- provide the individual/group with constructive feedback on performance;
- give the individual an opportunity to comment on own performance; and
- make provision for adjustments to performance objectives or measures if necessary.

There should be some kind of written account of the outcomes of the performance review, which can then be discussed at the individual's appraisal or used to make adjustments to performance, objectives or measures.

The appraisal system

In many organisations, the formal appraisal is an annual event since it takes up a considerable amount of the manager's time – or should do if it is being conducted effectively. Checklist 5.2 gives a number of reasons why it is necessary to hold an appraisal. As you read through the list, consider which of the functions your appraisal of others and your own appraisal fulfil.

Checklist 5.2   Why have appraisals?

- to identify and discuss an individual's current level of performance
- to identify training and development needs
- to provide an opportunity for giving and receiving feedback
- to assist in the allocation of rewards
- to give recognition for good performance
- to enable individuals to consider ways of improving performance
- to motivate individuals
- to construct succession plans
- to clarify and agree priorities and objectives
- to improve communication
- to identify potential performance
- to check on the effectiveness of personnel systems
- to discuss career options

Not all appraisals will be designed to fulfil all these functions, and it is often argued that appraisals should not be about the allocation of rewards, promotion or potential, or the collection of information to aid succession and human resource planning, but about improving working relationships. However, it is difficult in practice to categorise the purposes like that since, as an individual's line manager, you would be expected to contribute information about that person's potential and skills to other parts of the organisation and to recommend those you thought worthy of promotion.

Figure 5.2 outlines the place of appraisal in the development of the individual in order to meet organisational objectives. In its business plan, the organisation determines what it wants to achieve and translates this into high-level objectives. In turn, these objectives are translated into departmental objectives and expected performance standards. Both departmental objectives and the task itself contribute to defining an individual employee's objectives and expected standard of performance – and these are the bases for

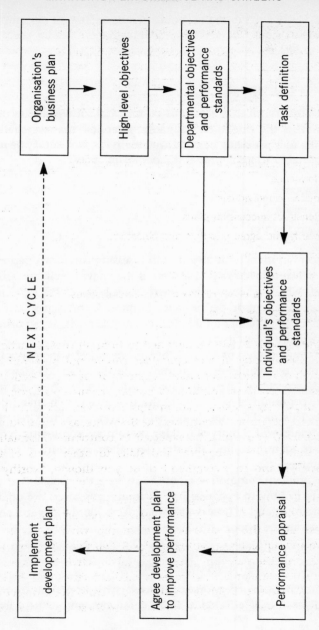

Figure 5.2 Developing people to meet organisational objectives

appraisal. As a result of the appraisal, a development plan for the individual should be agreed and implemented before the next cycle begins.

Methods of appraisal

There are a number of methods of appraisal, of which the most common is the one-to-one appraisal interview that we shall be covering in more detail below. Other methods, which may be used to contribute to an appraisal interview, include:

- self-appraisal
- peer review
- upward appraisal

Self-appraisal involves individuals in assessing their own performance, which is made easier for them if they have specific measures against which to rate their own contribution. *Peer appraisal* requires comment on performance from one's colleagues, and is a less popular appraisal method. People complain that it can disrupt close working relationships.

Becoming more common is *upward appraisal* which involves subordinates completing a questionnaire that asks for views on various aspects of their superior's performance. These are not usually communicated directly to the appraisee but collated into a report. This method has problems, however, since it is felt that subordinates will be wary of making meaningful comments in case they are identified, and superiors feel their authority could be undermined.

One problem common to all of the above is the probable lack of training in how to appraise; not all formal appraisers are offered such training, and so how could you expect subordinates and peers to be given the opportunity?

The paperwork for an appraisal interview

The amount of paperwork connected with appraisals can be considerable – Clive Fletcher (1993) comments on '... the universally applied, personnel-driven, standard procedure that stays rigidly in place (perhaps kept there by the weight of its own paperwork)'. Unfortunately, initiatives like Investors in People (IiP) seem to have re-created paperwork in a search for objectivity and record keeping. However, a relatively simple set of documents can be created that cover most eventualities and issues.

The first of these is a self-appraisal form, which the individual is asked to complete and send a copy to the appraiser before the appraisal interview. Checklist 5.3 outlines the kinds of questions which might be asked on a self-appraisal form.

Checklist 5.3 Self-appraisal form

(1) What have been your most important achievements since your last appraisal?

(2) What objectives/tasks did not go so well or were not completed? Can you give reasons for these?

(3) What training and development activities have you undertaken since your last appraisal?

(4) In which areas do you think it would be beneficial to develop your skills and competencies further?

(5) Are there any other areas in which you feel the job could be improved?

(6) In what ways could I or other managers help to improve the job?

(7) What career moves are you considering in (a) the short term and (b) the long term?

(8) What training and development might be useful in making such moves?

(9) What objectives would you set yourself for the next 12 months? (Please give main tasks involved, with their timescales, and suggest any performance measures that might be appropriate.)

These questions start off on a positive note, asking about achievements before going on to look at areas of improvement. At all points, the appraisee is given a chance to suggest ways in which performance or the job itself might be improved. Question (7) raises the issue of the individual's career aspirations and how these might be furthered. The final question about objectives would be a basis for discussion and agreement between the appraisee and the manager.

In addition to a copy of a self-assessment form completed by the appraisee, you should have the following other documents to hand for an appraisal interview:

- the previous appraisal document, setting out the agreed objectives at that time
- any reports from performance reviews
- any relevant reports from other managers, peers, subordinates
- any results from assessment centre activities or training courses

Training for appraisers

As I said earlier, few managers receive any training in appraisal interviewing and it is worth asking for this at your own appraisal. Such training usually involves some work on questioning techniques and some practice at appraisal interviewing.

Questioning techniques will be covered in more detail in Chapter 10, but for an appraisal your aim should be to let the appraisee talk for the majority of the time. Use the active listening technique described in Chapter 2 to facilitate and encourage this. Use the questions in the self-appraisal form to give structure to your interview.

Training in appraisal interviewing also involves reacting to scenarios like the ones below and considering how you would cope with each situation. Read through them and think about how you might handle them.

Example 1

Colin has only sketchily filled in his self-appraisal form and given no indication of objectives for next year. You know from his performance review reports that he has only been performing adequately and sometimes below what is expected of him. When he comes in for his interview, he is very defensive and monosyllabic.

Example 2

Joanne is one of your star performers, keen and enthusiastic about her job. However, she is slapdash and careless about certain aspects of it – the more boring form-filling and routine parts. She is obviously expecting promotion in the near future, but you are afraid her performance record does not warrant this.

Example 3

Andy starts off the interview by complaining vehemently about the performance of one of his team members, stating that it is lowering overall team performance.

Example 4

Corinne is in trouble. Her performance ratings are reasonable but she is suspected of falsifying some of the computer data to artificially inflate her results. Your supervisor reported this to you formally just before her appraisal interview and has told Corinne what he has done.

In the first case, you would need to encourage Colin to talk and to explain why he is underperforming. You would have the evidence to show him in his performance review reports but, remember, an appraisal interview is about improving performance, not about criticising it. You should aim to get him to suggest ways in which, with your help and support, his performance could be enhanced.

In the second case, it is only your – informed – opinion that Joanne would not get promotion as soon as she hopes. Your aim here is to convince her that she needs to pay more attention to the parts of her job that she is currently neglecting if she really wants promotion. You can also offer her training and development to further her ambitions.

The next two scenarios are really traps. An appraisal interview is not the place to raise a formal grievance and you should tell Andy that. It would be helpful to arrange a specific time to see him about his complaints, reminding him of the procedures for raising a formal grievance. Similarly, in the case of Corinne, an appraisal is not the place for a first-stage disciplinary interview, which should be left to another occasion.

The interview location

An appraisal interview is important and its location and timing should be protected. Checklist 5.4 outlines some of the factors you should consider when arranging the interview.

Checklist 5.4 Appraisal interviews: timing and location

- Held at a time and place as convenient to the appraisee as they are to you.
- The appraisee knows of the date, time and place well before the interview.
- The appraisee has had time to complete and return a self-appraisal form.
- The duration of the interview should be between one and two hours.
- The location is private and free from interruptions or distractions such as:
  - incoming telephone calls
  - casual visitors
  - undue external noise
  - excessive heat/cold
- You should not sit behind a desk in an authoritarian position.
- Refreshments (e.g. coffee) are available if wanted.

Below are some reports from appraisees whose appraisers obviously did not take the process seriously enough.

Example 5

'I'd just got back from a sales trip and met my manager in the corridor. He told me Head Office were making a fuss because he hadn't got round to appraising any of us yet and could I go to his office in half an hour for my appraisal. It really wasn't convenient because I had reports to write up if I was going to get away by six o'clock. I went along half-an-hour later and he wasn't there. His secretary said he'd just popped out and she'd ring me when he got back – that was twenty minutes later. He was in quite a state – he'd lost some vital figures or something and he'd lost my last year's appraisal form. Fortunately I had a copy. He asked me a few questions such as how was I getting on, did I have any problems, and what were my targets like? But most of the time he was searching for those wretched figures – he never did find them and, as far as I'm concerned, I never had my appraisal.'

Example 6

'My manager's a real nit-picker. When it came to discussing my work at my appraisal, he homed in on this one thing, the time I'd forgotten to send in a report because I'd been too busy and there'd been two of the team off sick. Couldn't let it go – on and on he went about it. Said it reflected badly on him. Nothing about how we achieved target over and over again. I went away feeling really fed up.'

Example 7

'Oh, yes – appraisal – well it's a bit of a farce really. George calls us in one at a time and tells us we're doing a great job and is there anything we want to ask him but he's got to go in ten minutes because he has an important appointment.'

Example 8

'My last appraisal was a non-event. I'd filled in the form very carefully and I really wanted to ask about jobs in Marketing – that's where I'd like to work. My manager left the door open so anyone passing could hear what was being said so I didn't like to bring the subject up. And then the phone – it just kept ringing and ringing. She didn't answer it, but it was really distracting and I couldn't remember half the things I wanted to say.'

The appraisal interview

We looked at management style in Chapter 1 and your style of approach to an appraisal interview is likely to affect its success. Maier (1959) identified three approaches to appraisal interviews, as follows:

- tell and sell – the manager tells the appraisee how he or she is performing and then tries to persuade the individual to accept what has already been decided in terms of improvement
- tell and listen – the manager tells the appraisee how he or she is performing but listens to the individual's viewpoint on the appraisal and training and development needs
- problem solving – the manager and appraisee reflect on performance and reach mutual decisions on how it might be improved

The first approach is rather autocratic and, if it involves much criticism, will have a negative effect on the appraisee. It can also be very difficult to persuade individuals to accept what has already been decided for them. The second approach at least involves the appraisee in the process of deciding on future action. The third approach is the favoured one, since the desired result is that the appraisee 'owns' the decisions about how to improve performance.

However, performance is only one of the topics to be discussed at an appraisal interview. If you go back to Checklist 5.3, you will see that I suggested questions on the self-appraisal form that covered training and development (past and future), improvements to the job itself, career planning and objective setting. In all cases, a problem-solving approach would be the most appropriate one to adopt. Your aim should be to produce an agreed development plan for each person you appraise.

After the interview

As soon as possible after the appraisal interview, you should produce a report, based on the self-appraisal form, that notes agreed outcomes and actions. The appraisee should have an opportunity to see this and to suggest any amendments before signing it. This record needs to be kept safely and in confidence. You also need to make any arrangements about agreed training and development opportunities and any other issues that you promised to follow up.

Evaluating an appraisal system

Like all systems, appraisal needs to be evaluated on a regular basis to see if it is meeting its objectives. It also needs to be cost-effective. Too often appraisal systems accumulate data that is never used or discarded. Sometimes, the information collected during an appraisal might be better collected in other ways. Undertaking appraisals can be very time-consuming for busy managers – perhaps the system is inefficient in this respect.

Checklist 5.5 lists some questions you should ask yourself as a manager and questions you should ask of your subordinates in relation to operating a cost-effective and efficient appraisal system. See how you would respond as a manager to the first set of questions about your own appraisal system.

Checklist 5.5 **Evaluating an appraisal system**

As a result of the appraisal system, do I:

- have a better understanding of the way in which my staff do their jobs?
- find it easier to appraise their performance?
- understand my staff better as individuals?
- find it easier to talk to them about job problems?
- find they come and discuss their job problems with me?
- find it easier to lead them?
- have a better working relationship with my staff?

From the appraisal system, do my staff:

- have a better understanding of their strong and weak points?
- find they are able to make a realistic assessment of their job performance?
- feel the appraisal has helped them to improve their job performance?

(adapted from *The Personnel Manager's Factbook*)

Are appraisals systems fair?

Despite every effort to design objective measures of performance, the appraisal system involves one human being judging another by using a mixture of objective measures and a good deal of subjective judgement. Banner and Cooke (1984) identified a number of what they considered to be ethical dilemmas in appraisals, including:

- the use of subjective criteria
- problems in defining performance standards and measurement indicators
- the use of different performance appraisal systems within the same organisation
- the uses to which information gained at an appraisal will be put
- who determines the objective standards to measure performance

Despite these concerns, the authors of the article concluded that 'As long as the performance appraisal *procedure* is fair, is consistent, and is evenly applied to all, the performance appraisal is a just device that can be morally justified' (Banner and Cooke, 1984, page 332.

However, it is not just the procedures and the system itself that can be in doubt. Longenecker and colleagues in 1987 in a survey of upper-tier managers found that over 70% of these managers deliberately inflated the ratings of their subordinates and would also deflate ratings intentionally. The reasons they gave for inflating ratings included:

- the belief that accurate ratings might damage subordinates' motivation and performance
- to increase the subordinate's eligibility for merit rises
- the desire to make the department shine in the eyes of others who might read appraisal reports
- to avoid giving the subordinate a negative record, which might affect his or her future

- to protect good performers going through a bad patch as a result of personal problems
- to reward employees who were making an effort even though their performance was still poor
- to avoid confrontation
- the desire to promote a poor or disliked employee out of the department

You would probably find yourself agreeing with some, if not all, of the reasons these senior managers gave for distorting the facts in an appraisal situation. However, they also reported deflating ratings on occasions – albeit less frequently than inflating them. The reasons they gave for deflating ratings included:

- to scare the employee into performing better
- to punish a difficult or rebellious employee
- to encourage a problem employee to leave
- to justify a planned firing
- to minimise the amount of merit pay a subordinate would receive
- to comply with an organisational edict which discouraged managers from giving high ratings

Would you agree that managers might be justified in deflating appraisal ratings or results for any of these reasons? How fair do you think your own appraisal system is – if you have one?

➡ CAREER MANAGEMENT

The whole area of career planning and management has shifted radically in the latter part of the twentieth century. Repeated de-layering and restructuring has meant there are fewer higher-level jobs which inhibits the promotion process. In many organisations, activities have been contracted out and more people are being employed on short-term, fixed-term and part-time contracts. Job security and clearly defined ladders of promotion are no longer the organisational norm. Today's high-flyers no longer see their careers as following a determinate path; rather, they see themselves as a collection of marketable skills and competencies, able to adapt swiftly to change. Where their older colleagues view redundancy with dread, these individuals see changing jobs and organisations, even with short periods of unemployment in between, as part of working life.

Example 1

Max and Donna both work in the software industry. In the past four years, Max has been made redundant twice and Donna three times. Apart from when Max was unemployed for three months, both of them have always found new, better-paid jobs within a week or two. On two occasions, Donna has been head-hunted. They are experts in their field and of considerable value to any company that employs them. The downside is that no company can expect their loyalty or commitment since they have no expectations of remaining in the same employment for more than a year or two.

Example 2

'We don't give people a career, we give them a job. Every day is an opportunity to prove that you should be given a chance or that your work is better than the next guy's. It is competitive. It is tough. No one is going to do you any favours. Ultimately, your own loyalty will be to yourself' (Tim Bell of the advertising agency Lowe, Howard-Spink and Bell).

Example 3

'You are asked to pour a part of yourself into the success of the company ... in many ways the individual is asked for a greater commitment than in the days when he or she was simply a cog in the wheel of a systematised corporation. In return, you should get an experience that sharpens your instincts, teaches you the newest lessons, shows you how to become self-engaged in your work, gives you new ways of looking at the world. ... I'm not asking for open-ended loyalty. I am asking people who are at Apple to buy into the vision of the company while they are here. ... The social contract is no longer valid. Nor, perhaps, should it be ... The trappings of loyalty – pension, cradle-to-grave employment – have been replaced by such things as creating opportunity, rewards and challenges for people' (John Sculley, President of Apple Computers, in 1987).

In their 1992 book *Smart Moves*, Golzen and Garner look at old myths about careers and the new realities, some of which are summarised below.

Myths	Realities
It is impossible for some institutions and organisations, because they are so large and stable, to change in the foreseeable future.	Look at the changes in public sector institutions, banks and other financial institutions in the UK due to privatisation and information technology.
You can't go wrong with growth areas of the economy or those with skill shortages.	New technologies can revolutionise production systems within a very short period; growth areas change; new skills are needed.
Qualifications are for ever.	The current trend is for continuous professional development (CPD) and updating, not a dependency on out-of-date qualifications.
It is a good sign when you can map your future in an organisation.	The only organisations where you can map your future are so stable as to be stagnant and at imminent risk of closure or takeover.
Success means getting to the top.	Success today is about self-development and self-actualisation, whether or not you reach the post of chief executive.

Your salary will rise annually so long as you perform adequately and don't make too many expensive mistakes.	More and more companies are bringing in performance-related pay.
Virtue and achievement will always be recognised in the end.	More and more organisations are buying in expertise from the outside, bringing with them new ideas and contacts, as well as costing little in training.
An internal promotion or upwards move is always a good thing.	Organisations now have much flatter hierarchies, and a sideways move may be more valuable, especially where performance is linked to pay.
It's all over when you reach age 50.	Those people with a wealth of experience are doing well as self-employed consultants, because of the increasing practice of contracting out all but core activities.

How do you feel after reading the last few paragraphs and the new realities identified by Golzen and Garner – depressed or enthused about your own career? And what can you do about it?

Training and development

Golzen and Garner (1992) stressed the reality that out-of-date and non-relevant qualifications were no longer the requirements for jobs and that new technologies meant people were constantly having to learn new skills. In the UK, the Institute of Management is looking at ways in which continuous professional development can be linked to the emerging National Record of Achievement that starts its life in the classroom. In our own research (Thomson et al., 1997), we found that a considerable number of managers who had obtained a Masters in Business Administration (MBA) qualification made a career move from large organisations into smaller companies or set up their own businesses, often because they felt blocked in the large organisation. The smaller organisation and the owner–manager business both benefit from the experience of these managers.

In your own appraisal and when appraising your staff, training and development should be high on the agenda. And not just training for the current job, but training to enhance your collection of skills so that you are ready for the next one.

Market intelligence

As you saw in Chapter 3, part of the manager's job is to forecast, and this can apply to career-related issues as well as to the job and the organisation. Knowing what your competitors are doing and how they are doing it is essential, for they may have invested in news processes, technologies or systems that will give them competitive edge. Being aware of new and more effective ways of doing the job means training yourself and your staff to meet new demands. If your current organisation is unwilling to move with the times, now is the time to invest in your own skill development and move yourself.

Being tempted to take the wrong job

Sometimes a career move appears to be so attractive that you fail to see what is behind it and that it is possibly a backward step in career terms. The money may be good and the job exciting – but will it lead anywhere? Will it enhance your marketability inside or outside the organisation?

Making yourself visible

Nobody gets noticed just by doing the job they are supposed to do, even if they are doing it well. Being 'visible' means taking the initiative so as to be noticed by senior management. Golzen and

Garner (1992) cite the example of the marketing manager who discovered there was a communications gap about what went on in his department. He initiated and sent out a weekly report of the department's activities, which, apart from being useful, got him noticed.

Becoming an expert

Today's valued employees are the 'knowledge workers' – people who collect, filter and distribute information as it is needed, enabling quick responses to be made to challenges and changes. Also valued are people who are experts in one or more areas and who can be called upon when their expertise is needed. Becoming an expert also involves being visible; the organisation has to know you exist.

The balance of responsibilities

Finally, consider the balance of responsibilities between you, the organisation and your staff for the management of their careers. The organisation has the responsibility to provide training and development opportunities and you have the responsibility for ensuring your staff know about them and have access to them. How your staff use those training and development opportunities is their responsibility; it is also your responsibility how you use the training and development opportunities offered to you. We will be discussing these opportunities in the next two chapters.

➡ CHRIS'S PROBLEM (5)

Delia had moved from your department to Chris's a year ago, which both of you saw as a good career move. Today she has asked to see you and tells you she was disappointed in her appraisal.

'I thought I'd done a really good job over the last year,' she tells you, 'but Chris didn't seem to think so. My supervisor thinks I'm after her job and she gave Chris a poor report on me. The trouble is, I haven't any way of proving that what she said was biased and, in some cases, downright untrue. Chris gave me a lecture about improving my performance and said I wasn't ready to go on that computer programming course I wanted until my supervisor was satisfied with my work. I just don't know what to do – I wish I'd never moved over there.'

What advice would you give to Chris about this situation?

References

Banner D. K. and Cook R. A., 'Ethical Dilemmas in Performance Appraisal' in *Journal of Business Ethics* (1984) Vol 3, pp. 327–33.

Fletcher C., 'Appraisals: an idea whose time has gone?' in *Personnel Management*, September 1993

Golzen G. and Garner A., *Smart Moves* (Penguin, London, 1992)

Longenecker C. O., Gioia D. A. and Sims H. P.' 'Truth or Consequences: Politics and Performance Appraisals' in *Business Horizons*, Nov/Dec 1987, pp. 1–7

Humble J. W., *Improving Business Results* (McGraw-Hill, Berkshire, 1967)

Koontz H., 'Making Sense of Management Theory' in *Harvard Business Review* (1962) Vol 40 No 4

Mabey C. and Salaman G., *Strategic Human Resource Management* (Blackwell, Oxford, 1995)

Maier N. R. F., *The Appraisal Interview* (Wiley, 1959)

Mento A. J., Steel R. P. and Karren R. I., 'A Meta-analytic Study of Task Performance: 1966–1984' in *Organisational Behaviour and Human Decision Processes* (1987) 39

Pearson R., *The Human Resource: Managing People and Work in the 1990s*, (McGraw-Hill Book Company (UK) Ltd., Berkshire, 1991)

Sculley J., *Odyssey: Pepsi to Apple* (Harper Row, London, 1987)

Thomson A., Storey J., Mabey C., Gray C., Farmer E. and Thomson R., *A Portrait of Management Development* (Institute of Management, London, 1997)

Chapter 6
Training and development

'We don't have, but we desperately need, a training culture.'

(Willis, 1989)

When Willis made this statement, it was true. One of the most comprehensive surveys of management development had been published two years earlier and had shown that the level of management training and development in the UK was much lower than in the US, Japan and the developed countries of Western Europe.

But the picture – as far as management training and development is concerned anyway – has changed. In 1997, Thomson et al. carried out another survey in the UK and found that:

- the priority given by organisations to management development had increased significantly in 1997 compared with ten years previously, and was expected to increase further in the foreseeable future; and

- only 4% of medium to large organisations and 20% of small organisations report doing no training, whereas in 1987 'somewhat over half of all UK companies appeared to make no formal provision for the training of their managers'.

Is this your experience? As a manager, have you received any or adequate training and development for your job and role? And to what extent do you get involved in the training and development of others? In this chapter, we will be looking at the way people learn and the environment of a 'learning organisation', as well as methods of training and development for yourself and your staff.

In the next chapter we will be looking more specifically at some ways in which you can train others.

Most people are fairly clear what they mean by 'training'. Training is usually directed towards acquiring specific skills, knowledge or competences related to a job or task (such as operating equipment, bookkeeping, marketing or sales). It involves changing or improving behaviour through learning to achieve effective performance.

'Development' is a wider concept and is related to future as well as current needs, as the following definition from Evenden and Anderson (1992) explains:

> Development involves enhancement, maturing, growing and improving what is already there. It can relate to any aspect of the individual that is capable of change and progression. At work, we think of this often in terms of the 'hard' skill and knowledge development directly related to the technical aspects of the job. ... It is also useful to consider personal growth as a very important factor in this process. Thus development can include personal factors like increasing understanding and self awareness; learning skills; perceived responsibility for self development; confidence and self image. These 'soft' personal factors not only affect the acquisition of the 'hard' skills, but directly influence motivation, commitment and capacity to make choices and achieve personal goals. (Evenden and Anderson, 1992)

➡ HOW PEOPLE LEARN

Training and development involve learning – learning new skills and new ways of doing things. But in the same way that individuals value different rewards, individuals also learn in different ways.

We know there are differences between the ways in which children and adults learn. From an early age, children are classroom-bound and what they are presented with to learn is decided for them – this is known as 'directed' learning. Experiments in self-directed learning for children have had very mixed results; some children are able to manage this approach but the majority are not and prefer dependency on the teacher.

Adults learners, on the other hand, usually choose what they want to learn and can take responsibility for their own learning. Some adults who have had bad experiences of learning as children have a number of barriers to overcome when it comes to learning as an adult; they see the whole process as one that will lead them to fail. Until they are motivated by some kind of valued outcome or reward to consider learning again, this barrier will never be broken down.

Many adult learners are also very instrumental. They are prepared to learn if they see the outcome as positive and related to their immediate needs. Look at the two examples of learning experiences below, which illustrate this.

Example 1

Damien's manager is very keen on training courses and thinks that everyone should take at least one course a year. In this way, he believes he will motivate his staff to improve their performance. At his appraisal, he tells Damien he wants him to go on an accounting course. 'It's for trainees, not accountants,' he explains to Damien, who looks rather bewildered at being sent on such a course since his job does not involve dealing with budgets or finance of any kind. The course lasted for six months and, at the end of it, Damien sat an examination and failed it.

His manager was furious. 'All that money wasted,' he fumed. 'Why didn't you try a bit harder?'

Damien shrugged. 'It wasn't interesting,' he said. 'Lots of figures and that, but you weren't allowed to use a spreadsheet – in fact I don't think the instructor had even heard of a computer. And it was all above my head anyway. It's not as if I was dealing with accounts at work, and I don't want to.'

Example 2

Jenny was very keen to be promoted and to move up to a junior management job. She badgered her manager about training courses in leadership and motivating people and about taking a qualification in management. Her manager was reluctant to send her on these courses as they had no relevance to the job she was doing at the moment. However, Jenny offered to pay half the cost of a Certificate in Management and her manager eventually agreed to her taking the course. She passed with flying colours, coming first in her year.

At her appraisal, her manager congratulated her and said, 'I suppose it was because you were putting up half the money yourself that spurred you on.' Jenny was stunned. She knew it wasn't the money; it was because she wanted to move into management – and she thought she would probably be a lot better at it than her manager was.

There is no point in forcing adults to learn for the sake of learning (or for the sake of the training statistics), as you can see from the first example. Adults need to see the relevance of the learning experience to their own needs and interests. This was why Jenny succeeded in the second example. Her goal was to move into management and she felt a qualification would be of help in that.

Adults are also able to undertake 'vocational' or 'experiential' learning, which is less common in the classroom. This type of learning is of direct practical use to them in their job and, because adults generally come ready-packaged with a wealth of experience, trainers and teachers of adults can tap this experience using a number of techniques such as role play, case studies, group discussions and problem-solving exercises.

Different learning styles

A considerable amount of research has gone into discovering how people learn, and I have summarised below two of these pieces of research work.

Honey and Mumford (1992) classified people as having a preferred learning style (but 'preferred' does not mean that they do not learn in other ways when necessary) as follows:

- activists – enjoy new experiences; are gregarious, open-minded and enthusiastic; thrive on challenge and need always to be busy
- reflectors – prefer to collect and analyse data; reflective and

observant; listen to others before making a carefully considered contribution

- theorists – logical and analytical, rational and objective
- pragmatists – keen on new ideas and how they work in practice, but tend to be impatient and like to get on with things; practical, down-to-earth

Pask and Scott (1972) categorised people with different learning styles as:

- serialists – learn, remember and recapitulate information in sequence; learn by small steps, trying to get each point clear before moving on to the next one
- holists – make an image of an entire system of facts or information, from which they derive what is relevant; tackle several ideas at once

Obviously, you would need to read much more than this on the subject of learning styles to understand them fully. But even from the brief descriptions given above, it is possible to see that, for example, a learning experience designed for activists would not be so effective with reflectors. Honey and Mumford (1992) suggest that the design of any training programme needs to be:

- practical enough for pragmatists
- soundly based for theorists
- novel for activists
- paced to suit the need of reflectors

➡ THE LEARNING ORGANISATION

The phrase 'the learning organisation' causes some confusion. It is argued that the learning organisation is not a tangible entity but rather a set of processes. A learning organisation is one that positively encourages learning as part of its culture. Checklist 6.1 outlines the elements of a learning organisation. As you read through it, think about your own organisation and to what extent it could be classified as a 'learning organisation'.

Checklist 6.1 Elements of a learning organisation

- There is a clear picture of how the organisation should operate.
- Employees at all levels understand the importance of both learning and doing.
- Employees are encouraged and rewarded for asking questions and challenging work practices.
- Systems exist to encourage entrepreneurial learning.
- Performance reviews and career development look at what employees have done and what they have learned.
- Compensation systems are offered that support the stated values of the organisation.
- Bonuses and incentives are balanced between current performance, innovation, courage and risk.
- Feedback systems guarantee ongoing information about what has been learned as well as what has been done; personal feedback is frequent and can be both negative and positive.
- Improvement is valued as much as results.
- Information systems are designed to manage the balance between learning and doing.
- Training and education programmes are designed to maximise the balance between learning and doing.
- A communication strategy exists to keep learning at the forefront of everyone's consciousness.
- A strategic planning process exists that is thought of as a learning as well as a doing process.
- Strategic objectives exist that are defined to include the learning that must take place in order to achieve them.

(adapted from Beckhard and Pritchard, 1992)

➡ DIAGNOSING TRAINING NEEDS

Too often, an organisation only wakes up to the need for training when a crisis occurs – such as an upturn in customer complaints or staff turnover. The kind of knee-jerk response usually made is to send everyone off on a training course, but, as we have seen, this is not the answer. The training has to be relevant not only to the organisation's needs but to the individual's needs as well.

A 'training needs analysis' involves auditing existing performance and skills and comparing these with the desired level of performance and skills in the future. With the pace of change in organisational environments at the moment, it is very likely that employees will need new skills if they are to perform adequately in the future.

The skills revolution

In 1993, a report by Gallie and White entitled *Employee Commitment and the Skills Revolution* was published by the Policy Studies Institute. This report stated that there had been a skills revolution within the last five years at all levels, such that 63% of skilled manual workers and 70% of non-manual workers reported that their work now required increased skills. This was mainly due to the rise in the use of computers and computer systems, although an increase in the skills of monitoring and of social skills was also reported. In general, employees reported an increase in their influence over their immediate work tasks (Hendry, 1995).

A further study, this time of managers, was commissioned by the Institute of Management (IM) in 1994. Managers also reported changes and increases in their skills and, like those interviewed in the earlier survey, stated that they felt they were working harder. The managers in the IM survey reported that they needed skills in:

- sensing and predicting change
- responding to and managing change
- strategic thinking
- thinking on their feet

- swift decision making
- managing risk
- tolerating failure
- being aware of the organisation as a whole
- self-developing
- finance
- information management and IT

As a manager, you have probably increased and changed your skills over the last five years and can expect to do so continually if the pace of change persists at its current rate. But you also need to keep up-to-date with the skills of your staff so as to ensure that they are adequate to meet the future demands of your organisation.

Carrying out a training needs analysis

As stated in the previous chapter, discussion of individual training needs can be one of the functions of appraisal interviews and performance reviews. It involves exploring the areas in which the individual feels he or she needs to improve, how best this improvement can be effected, and whether or not training is one of the methods that might be used. However, analysing training needs must not just be related to improvement in the current job but to the future skills that the organisation will need if it is to grow and survive. This is where your skill in sensing and predicting the future becomes necessary.

There are a number of ways of conducting a training needs analysis, and Checklist 6.2 gives some of these. You might like to think about which of them would be appropriate in your case. Some of the methods are discussed in more detail below.

Checklist 6.2 **Methods of collecting data for analysing training needs**

- appraisal forms and interviews
- performance reviews

- job analysis
- questionnaires
- staff records
- development centres
- business simulations
- psychometric tests.

Job analysis

This will be discussed in more detail in Chapter 9 in relation to recruitment and selection. However, in the consideration of training needs and in particular those for the future, it is useful to take a fresh look at the job itself. Job descriptions are often outdated and rather vague; the job may have changed by becoming enriched, or it may require new skills in the use of technology; it may require to be changed because the method of carrying out the job might be improved. Looking at the job and how it might be performed in the future can give you a basis for identifying any skill changes required by those doing the job.

Questionnaires

Sending out questionnaires about training needs is a cheap and effective method of collecting data, especially when you want to survey a large number of employees. The data can usually be easily summarised and provide the basis for designing a training and development programme but, as a method of identifying individual training needs, it would be preferable to support the data with personal interviews.

Staff records

These can be a valuable source of data about training already undertaken (as long as they are accurate and up-to-date!), providing you with information about the type and level of training or development activity undertaken. You may also find that someone has undertaken training in a particular skill area or for a specific job which is currently unrelated to the job they are performing. These skills might be built upon for future job needs.

Development centres

These can be used for identifying training and personal development needs, but they are not a viable option unless your organisation already operates development-centre assessment since they are costly to set up and run. A development centre is not a place; it is a collection of methods designed to assess performance. It can be used to heighten self-awareness of strengths and weaknesses in relation to possible future jobs, and as the basis for a training and development programme for the individual.

Business simulations

These are relatively expensive to run and more often used for senior executive development programmes. They involve participants in undertaking a role in a fictional business, and are usually administered by trained psychologists. After the simulation itself, each participant is interviewed by the psychologist who gives that person confidential feedback on his or her performance, enabling the individual to identify strengths and weaknesses.

Psychometric tests

Although more often used for determining personality factors in recruitment and assessment, some tests can be used to pinpoint development needs in particular. There is the Career Anchors Inventory, for example, which can be used to identify work and career aspirations and attitudes. Any psychometric test, however, should only be administered and interpreted by a trained psychologist.

Analysing training needs is the second step in the training and development cycle that is shown in Figure 6.1. The first step – monitor performance – is related to what was discussed in the previous chapter on performance measurement and management: if someone is performing below standard, it may or may not be a training or development shortfall.

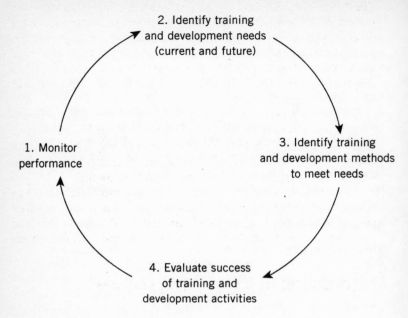

Figure 6.1 The training and development cycle

Having identified that there is a need for training and development which should improve performance, the next step is to consider what method(s) would be most appropriate to meet the identified needs.

➡ METHODS OF TRAINING AND DEVELOPMENT

There are a large number of methods of training and developing staff, some of which can be undertaken inside the organisation and some requiring day (or longer) release from work. Your choice of methods will depend on the extent to which your organisation is able to offer formal in-house training, whether or not it has a training department, and whether or not you need to rely on external sources such as consultants or institutions.

In general, the responsibility for training and development

should be a shared one: the organisation has a responsibility to provide the methods for internal training or the financing for external programmes, while the individual has the responsibility for undertaking these development opportunities to the best of his or her ability. Training and development in the UK nowadays has a much higher profile than it did in the mid-eighties, and needs to be seen as a partnership.

Checklist 6.3 lists a variety of training and development methods, some of which are expensive in terms of time and money, some of which are relatively inexpensive. You might like to think about which methods your organisation currently provides and which additional methods you feel would be useful.

We shall be looking at the first four methods in Checklist 6.3 in much more detail in the next chapter, since these are ones that you as a manager can carry out internally. Job enrichment was discussed in Chapter 4. Some of the other methods in the list are discussed below.

Checklist 6.3   Methods of training and development

- induction
- coaching
- mentoring
- delegating
- job enrichment
- job rotation
- job shadowing
- on-the-job learning
- external courses
- seminars
- workshops
- computer-based programmes
- business games/simulations
- videos
- development centres
- qualifications

- technical training
- secondment
- conferences
- visits
- special assignments or projects
- case studies and role plays
- discussions
- guided learning (e.g. open/distance learning)
- learning resource centres

Depending on whether or not the organisation has an internal training department, the above list can be subdivided into internal and external methods of development as I suggested earlier. It can also be further subdivided into formal and informal methods of training although, even here, the subdivision can get blurred.

Formal methods of training and development would normally include any planned and structured programme of activities provided by the organisation for its employees, such as job rotation, workshops, development centre activities, technical training, qualifications, secondment, visits and projects. Informal methods are less planned and structured and might include coaching, delegating, job enrichment, job shadowing, and learning on the job. Perhaps one of the ways to distinguish between the formal and informal is the extent to which the training and development activity is formally evaluated.

In the survey by Thomson et al. (1997), the most frequently mentioned informal method of management training and development was learning on the job. While this might seem a relatively inexpensive method, it has obviouis drawbacks in that the learning curve could be quite extended. It is certainly experiential, but it does not necessarily produce a high level of performance – it depends on how you 'do the job' and how you learn to do it. Look at the example below.

Example 3

Tess has been promoted to a management post from being a

technical supervisor. Although she had already had some experience of managing staff, it had been at a fairly low level since she
had reported any underperformance or other problems to her
manager, who then dealt with them. In the first few weeks in her
new role, she managed to upset two members of staff, one of whom
made a formal complaint about her. She had no idea how to handle
a budget and was terrified of overspending. Consequently, she cut
back in some areas where this was inadvisable, creating more
problems for herself and her staff. At meetings she rarely spoke up
as she was often unsure of her position or what the other managers
were discussing. Eventually, she became so demoralised that she
had to take extended sick leave for a stress-related illness.

All too often, people like Tess, whether they are managers or not,
are left to sink or swim by learning on the job. No one has been
assigned to coach or mentor them, and everyone else seems too
busy to give advice. It is a true baptism of fire!

For the organisation that does not have an internal training
department, external courses would seem to be the only alternative. But not only are these courses expensive, they are also costly
in terms of time lost to the organisation when the individuals are
away from their place of work. Since most do not offer assessment,
it is often difficult to evaluate their quality apart from through
improved performance or skill acquisition when the person comes
back to work and puts the learning into practice. Another problem
associated with external courses can be the 're-entry' problem:
unless the course is directly relevant to the individual's current job,
it may be difficult to put the learning into practice back in the
workplace.

Job rotation and job shadowing

Job rotation and job shadowing tend to be relatively effective
methods. Job rotation is particularly useful for team or project
work, where members spend some time doing the jobs of others.
This raises awareness of each person's role in the team as well as
creating greater flexibility and skills within the team as a whole.
Job shadowing can be beneficial if either the jobholder who is
moving on or someone else performing a similar job is available.

However, you have to remember that these people are not trained trainers and that they may pass on bad as well as good practice.

Seminars and conferences

Seminars and conferences are more often used as development opportunities by middle and senior managers, who are interested in the strategic management of organisations or in a particular aspect of managerial responsibility such as managing change, re-engineering, or organisational development.

Visits

By 'visits' in Checklist 6.3, I mean planned visits to, or meetings with, customers or clients or suppliers or other people in the organisation. In this way, the trainee gains other perspectives on his or her role and can set it in context. Special assignments and projects also need to be organised. These should involve acquiring new skills or competences through working with others as well as bringing the individual's own special skills to the assignment or project.

Case studies, role plays and group discussions

The first two of these methods are frequently used by trainers to give trainees an opportunity to explore a problem or a situation. It can be an active learning experience that many trainees value because it lets them try out ideas and possible solutions in a non-threatening environment. Case studies in particular are a flexible method that can be used with both individuals and groups. In the latter situation, there are also considerable learning opportunities in the areas of group dynamics, teamworking and decision making. Similarly, role plays allow participants to try out skills such as interviewing, negotiating and counselling in a risk-free setting, with the provision of constructive feedback.

Group discussions, either as part of a training and development programme or run by the manager at work, are an opportunity to share ideas and experience and can be a valuable learning activity, especially for new members of staff.

Learning resource centre

Even small organisations can have a 'Learning resource centre'. This is a place where staff can come and look at training and development opportunities both inside and outside the organisation. It might, for example, contain:

- samples of materials from external providers (e.g. local colleges, open learning)
- books
- manuals
- details of courses run in-house and outside.

A learning resource centre can put more responsibility on the individual to find something that suits their particular needs.

➡ DESIGNING AND EVALUATING TRAINING AND DEVELOPMENT PROGRAMMES

As we have seen, training and development programmes need to be specifically designed to meet individual needs, and they may consist of one or more training or development activities undertaken inside or outside the organisation. But the programmes also need to be evaluated to ensure that they are meeting the individual's and the organisation's objectives.

The first step in designing and evaluating a training programme is to discuss it thoroughly with the employee(s) concerned. In this way, you can clarify that the programme is relevant to their needs, is at the right level and has relevant content. It also lets your staff know that you are interested in their training and development and gives them an opportunity to discuss with you any concerns they have about it. It is an opportunity for you and your staff to think about ways in which training or development can be put into practice after the event, what feedback the individual will give you on the training activity, and how you will be evaluating the training and monitoring performance. Part of this discussion should also focus on the rewards the training should bring the person concerned. These might be intrinsic rewards such as a sense of achievement at acquiring new skills or more tangible rewards such as a salary increase or promotion.

Armstrong (1991) identifies the following topics which you as a manager need to consider when designing a training programme:

- the objectives of the programme
- its content
- its length
- where it will take place
- what methods will be used
- who will provide the training

to which I would add:

- how the programme will be evaluated.

There area number of features of a training and development programme that can be evaluated, the majority of which are given in Checklist 6.4.

Checklist 6.4 **Features of training programmes that can be evaluated**

- the outcomes of the programme
- the training staff
- the trainee's reactions
- the learning methods used
- materials used
- course content and structure
- the trainee/development process
- the value of the programme to:
  - a trainee
  - the job itself
  - the organisation

Ideally, the outcomes of the programme should have been

determined when the method of training and development is selected. If you decide to send one of your staff on a course, you need to clarify both for yourself and the trainee what outcomes you expect from it.

Example 4

In order to illustrate how training and development can be designed and evaluated, we can look at the case of Jane, a new recruit to a sales team. She comes from a public relations company but has had no experience of direct sales. Your objectives in this case would be to provide a programme of training and development that will equip her to become an effective member of your sales team. Below is an outline programme of training and development for Jane. As you read through the outline, think about the methods you might use and how the programme might be evaluated.

Sales training and development programme

Company and product knowledge

Sales administration

Knowledge of customers

Knowledge of competitors

Communication skills

Presentation skills

Handling complaints

Closing a sale

Record-keeping

The first set of outcomes you would be looking for would be company and product knowledge and sales administration. In order to fulfil these outcomes, you might set up a series of workshops and visits within your organisation so that she becomes familiar with the products she is going to sell and knowledgeable about the company itself and how sales are processed and administered. You might also provide her with background information in the form of publicity material, specifications, manuals of procedures, the company's mission statement and its latest annual report. You would be able to evaluate the outcomes of this training through testing her knowledge, either through questioning or through a written paper.

Job shadowing would be an appropriate technique for getting to know customers. Jane could accompany an experienced salesperson on visits and not only learn about the customers but also pick up some sales techniques. However, that person would need to have had some training in coaching if he or she was required to act as a 'trainer' as well as a salesperson. Again, Jane's knowledge about customers could be tested after the visits had taken place. To complement her visits and learning, she should also attend any meetings of the sales team and be encouraged to ask questions and contribute her own ideas from an early stage.

Knowledge of competitors would require her to know about other similar products and the competitive advantage of what she is selling, which might be its price, its high quality, its wide availability, its fast delivery time and so on. To evaluate her learning, you might ask Jane to write you a report about the competitive advantages of the product she is selling over other similar products.

So far, Jane's training has taken place within the organisation, using other members of its staff to familiarise her with the company, its products, its administration, its customers and its competitors. The other training needs identified in the outline programme are concerned with the skills that Jane needs to acquire in order to become a successful salesperson.

At this point you might decide to go outside the company and find specialist skills training unless you have an internal training department that can cover the areas you have identified. Even if you do use internal trainers, the training should be evaluated. Today, the trend is for organisations to contract out training and development to their training department in much the same way as outside providers, charging the organisation's department for their services. They can be in competition with these outside providers in some cases, or they can collaborate with them by contracting *in* some of their staff for specialist training needs.

In Jane's case, let's assume there is no internal training provision, which means finding relevant courses within your training budget and within the timescale you have set for her training. These may be provided by local consultants or training companies, business schools, higher or further education colleges, training and education councils (TECs) or similar organisations. Your choice would depend on what was available and the extent to which any course met Jane's training needs. To help you in your choice (assuming you had one), you should ask about the background of the people undertaking the training, what methods they use, and how they and the programme itself would be evaluated by the provider.

Measures you might use to evaluate the people who are directing the training include:

- their qualifications
- their experience
- their skills in transferring learning

How long has the institution or individual been in the business of training? Are the staff a good advertisement for the training they offer – particularly when you are looking for training in communication and presentation skills? Have they first-hand experience of, for example, closing a sale or handling complaints? Or are they merely failed salespeople who are likely to pass on bad practice? Are they using up-to-date, relevant training methods that will appeal to a range of learning styles? Are training objectives set and met?

Training in communication and presentation skills should involve the opportunity for trainees to participate as much as possible and to practise the skills they are acquiring. The use of role play, for example, in communications skills training is effective. Closed-circuit television is particularly useful in letting individuals see their bad habits and helping them to get rid of them. Making presentations of different lengths is vital; you can't just expect a trainee to absorb the learning without the opportunity to practise in front of others. Similarly, in the area of interpersonal skills in handling complaints and closing a sale, role play and short scenarios are effective training methods.

Obviously, one method of evaluation of external training and development is to gather the trainees' reactions. Did they find the activity useful? What were their impressions of the training staff and the programme as a whole? Did they enjoy the experience?

What have they learned? How do they expect to put what they have learned into practice? Answers to questions like these will provide you with information about the programme, its staff, its methods, content and materials. To complete the feedback loop, this information should be passed back to the training providers to help them improve their programmes. Too often, trainees are asked to fill in 'happy sheets' at the end of a course, which are returned to the training staff and often ignored. These sheets tend to be skewed towards the 'popular' trainer, the person who is friendly and outgoing and, probably, genuinely interested in the trainees – but who may be using out-of-date training methods and concepts.

Finally, Jane needed training in record keeping, which could be undertaken through an externally provided course although the training might not be specific enough for her needs. Any general course of this kind would need to be complemented by some internal coaching on the particular ways in which the organisation expected its records to be kept, its deadlines for returns, its invoice processing etc.

At each stage of the training, I have suggested ways in which it might be evaluated. However, the major evaluation will come after the training is completed and Jane puts it all into practice, for this is where the value of the training and development programme as a whole needs to be assessed. This is also the fourth stage in the training and development cycle. You could assess Jane's performance in a number of ways:

- through personal observation of her performance
- through reported observation by someone allocated to her as a coach
- through her sales figures against sales targets
- through reports from customers

Monitoring performance after training and development is essential in order to determine whether a programme is effective and whether individuals learned appropriate knowledge and skills. As the diagram of the Training and Development Cycle (Figure 6.1) shows, this monitoring process feeds back into the identification of further training and development needs.

Training records

Particularly if you have no Personnel Department, you need to keep records of training. In addition, even if you do work in an organisation where the responsibility for organising training rests with someone else, you need to keep that person informed about process and progress. When an appraisal is carried out, you should record the individual's training needs and either follow these up yourself or pass them on to the person responsible for training in your organisation. When the next appraisal comes round, the training needs and training record provide a check on how the individual is progressing and what training has been undertaken.

A training record should include details of all courses and formal or informal methods of training undertaken by the individual, as well as any feedback from that person on the learning experience.

➡ CHRIS'S PROBLEM (6)

Chris tells you with satisfaction that, for once, the department is going to be ahead of the field. 'Have you seen the memo from Head Office,' Chris asks you, 'the one about the new records system they're going to put in next year? Well, it's a pretty quiet period for us just now and a friend of mine has just started up his own training business, specialising in computer systems, so I'm going to send everyone in the department on his training course. Then, when the new records system comes in, we'll be the only department where everyone has already been trained. I can see promotion on the horizon for this one.'

How would you deter Chris from following up on this idea?

References

Armstrong M., *A Handbook of Personnel Management Practice*, 4th edn (Kogan Page, London, 1991)

Beckhard R. and Pritchard W., *Changing the Essence: The Art of Creating and Leading Fundamental Change in Organisations* (Jossey-Bass, San Francisco 1992)

Management Development to the Millennium: the Cannon and Taylor Working Party Reports (Institute of Management, London, 1994)

Evenden R. and Anderson G., *Management Skills: Making the Most of People* (Addison-Wesley, Wokingham, 1992) p. 287

Gallie D. and White M., *Employee Commitment and the Skills Revolution* (Policy Studies Institute, London, 1993)

Hendry C., *Human Resource Management: a Strategic Approach to Employment*, (Butterworth Heinemann, Oxford, 1995)

Honey P. and Mumford A., *The Manual of Learning Styles* (Peter Honey, 1992)

Pask G. and Scott B. C. E., 'Learning Strategies and Individual Competence', *International Journal of Man–Machine Studies* (1972) Vol 4

Thomson A., Storey J., Mabey C., Gray C., Farmer E. and Thomson R., *A Portrait of Management Development* (Institute of Management, London, 1997)

Willis N., 'A Worker's Right to Train', *National Westminster Bank Quarterly Review*, February 1989

Chapter 7

Induction, coaching, mentoring and delegating

'Doing a job is more difficult than telling someone else how the job ought to be done.'

(C Northcote Parkinson, 1959)

The quotation above is a cynical comment on those people who are always ready to tell you how any job, including your own, should be done. And, sometimes, it *is* easier to tell someone how a job ought to be done than actually doing it. Some of the training and development methods in this chapter involve 'telling' people how a job ought to be done, but telling them in a structured way through coaching, mentoring and delegating.

The topics in this chapter are all methods of training and development that you as a manager are likely to be involved in. The induction of a new member of staff should be your responsibility, or at least a shared responsibility with your Personnel Department if you have one. Coaching and mentoring are developmental activities that you may undertake yourself or may allocate to other people in your area of managerial responsibility. And delegation should be seen more as a developmental opportunity for your staff than as a workload release for yourself.

➡ DESIGNING AN INDUCTION PROGRAMME

When a new member of staff joins your department or team, that person needs to become familiar with the organisation and how it works as well as undertaking any training for the job itself. There are a number of ways in which this information can be passed on to the individual, including:

- the written terms and conditions of employment
- the written job description
- the contract of employment
- the company handbook or other documents such as company policy on smoking in the workplace, health and safety, grievance and disciplinary procedures
- access to a mentor during the first weeks/months of employment

Like any other training activity, induction needs to be planned with the particular information needs of the individual in mind. Someone who has transferred in from another part of the organisation, for example, is unlikely to need much, if any, induction in the organisation itself and how it works.

A new employee, however, has a lot to learn and there is the danger of information overload if the induction process is not planned over a specific timescale. Look at Checklist 7.1, which outlines the kinds of information a new employee will need within the first few weeks of employment, and think about how you might structure an induction programme that delivers relevant and appropriate information over that period.

Checklist 7.1   **Induction information for new employees**

- when and where to arrive
- terms and conditions of employment
- where he/she is going to work
- who he/she is going to work with
- line management, supervision and other reporting lines
- how wages/salary will be paid
- expenses arrangements for travel and subsistence
- pension and insurance schemes
- how long the probation period is (if appropriate)

- holiday entitlement/rota system
- sickness − notification of absence, certificates, pay
- where the basic amenities − lavatories, cloakrooms, canteen − are located
- hours of work and official breaks
- what the job entails
- how the job relates to other jobs
- what is expected (quality standards)
- Health and Safety regulations
- medical and first-aid facilities
- procedures for making a grievance
- organisational rules and procedures for disciplinary action
- what training is available/necessary to perform the job
- promotion opportunities and procedures
- union and joint consultation agreements
- the organisation's structure, policies, goals, mission statement, products or services etc.
- cultural norms − 'the way we do things around here

As you can see, the list is a long one and there may be additional organisation-specific information that you might want to include. Induction is time-consuming, but worth the effort as the individual will quickly become productive.

Armstrong (1991) defines the aims of induction as:

- to smooth the preliminary stages when the new employee is likely to find everything strange and unfamiliar
- to establish quickly a favourable attitude to the company in the mind of the new person so that he or she is more likely to stay
- to obtain effective performance from the new employee in the shortest possible time

Planning the first day

Someone needs to meet the new employee and take responsibility for the first day at work. This person should be a responsible and knowledgeable person, well briefed and with a schedule of events that the new employee is expected to attend. A suggested plan for a new employee's first day is given below, where the person's line manager has taken the overall responsibility for its design but has involved others in its implementation.

Induction Programme for new member of staff

Before Day 1

Ensure the new member of staff (Karen) knows to come to the reception desk in the main office at 8.30 a.m. on 1 September and to ask for Jo Carter.

Alert reception that a new member of staff will be arriving at that time and date.

Ensure that other members of staff involved in the induction programme are clear about their duties and timings.

Check with Barry (supervisor) that all equipment is in place and working and that he has set a number of specific tasks for Karen to undertake during her first week.

Have all the necessary documents available:
- terms and conditions of employment
- rules and regulations
- map of site
- organigram
- employee handbook (if there is one).

Arrange for refreshments, lunch etc.

Day 1

08.30   Meet Karen in my office (coffee available).

        Check she has received her contract of employment and is clear about this.

        Check personal information – who to contact in an emergency etc.

        Outline programme for the day.

Ask if she has any immediate concerns or questions. Introduce her to my PA, who will show her where the amenities are.

09.00 Introduce her to Barry, who will be be Karen's supervisor, and to Gail, who will be her mentor. Barry to outline the requirements of the job and introduce her to the other members of the team.

10.00 Coffee break with team members – Barry to introduce Karen and explain where she fits in to the team.

10.20 Gail to take Karen through the stages of the job, check she is familiar with the equipment and whether she needs any training to operate it effectively. Explain safety precautions and procedures. Ensure she knows what tasks she is expected to undertake during her first week. Ensure she knows that Gail will be her first point of contact if she has any problems.

11.00 Work practice under supervision.

12.00 Gail to take Karen to lunch in the staff canteen, show her around and answer any questions.

13.00 Gail to take her to meet Frances in Finance. Frances to explain system for paying wages, sick pay, holiday pay, bonuses and expenses.

13.30 Gail to bring Karen to my office. Check her initial reactions – any questions, concerns at this point? Arrange any training if necessary.

14.00 Work practice under supervision.

16.30 Meeting with Gail to discuss other induction activities.

Quite an exhausting day, and one in which a number of people have been involved in passing on information to the new person. Most of this has been to do with the job itself and with essential facts about the layout of the buildings, pay and basic amenities. Some of Karen's time has been spent actually performing tasks that will be part of her job so that she can become familiar with what is expected of her. What next?

Induction Programme for new member of staff (contd)

(NB: if special initial training is required, this will take place on Day 2 if possible.)

Day 2
Morning: job practice under supervision.
Afternoon: Gail to take Karen on a tour of building and introductions to other staff in Marketing and Production Departments.

Day 3
Morning: job practice.
Afternoon: Barry to go through organisation's rules (e.g. Health and Safety) and give Karen copies of any relevant documents (arrange time to suit).

Day 4
All day: job practice.

Day 5
Morning: job practice and team meeting.

14.00 My office: explanation of how Karen's job and the work of the unit fits into the organisation as a whole. Tell her about the history of the organisation, its values and its mission. Ask about any questions and concerns.

By the end of the first working week, the new employee has not only had plenty of opportunities to get to grips with the job but she has also been given a lot of information. The induction process is by no means complete, however, and her mentor and her manager should arrange regular meetings with her to ensure she has settled in and to identify any problems she is encountering.

➡ **COACHING**

Coaching is a role you may decide to take on yourself or one that you feel might be better carried out by someone else. It involves helping another person to develop their skills and knowledge –

passing on your experience to someonie else rather as masters did to apprentices in the past. It should be a rewarding experience for both the coach and the learner; if it is not, then the coaching is not being effective.

Coaching is time-consuming and it requires certain skills such as:

- understanding the learner's preferred learning style
- developing a relationship of mutual trust and respect
- developing the learning skills of the learner
- encouraging the learner to seek their own solutions
- finding and designing learning situations
- giving balanced and constructive feedback

Before taking on a coaching role, or asking someone else to undertake it, you need to consider whether you or the other person can invest protected and uninterrupted time with the learner and whether you (or the other person) have the necessary coaching skills. Perhaps this would be an opportunity to suggest at your next appraisal that you need some training in coaching. Below are two examples of how different managers approached the coaching role.

Example 1

Megan had been asked by her manager to help Jean, a new member of staff, by coaching her in her job as supervisor. To be honest, Megan had no idea what 'coaching' meant and her manager was equally vague. 'Just keep an eye on her,' was his suggestion. 'If she has any problems, see if you can sort things out for her – that sort of thing.'

Full of good intentions, Megan told Jean that she had been assigned to coach her in her new job, which seemed to surprise Jean since this was the first she had heard of it. Megan painstakingly went through all the facets of the job and what Jean was supposed to do and not do as a supervisor. Jean didn't appear to have any questions so Megan felt she had done a good job.

'Come along and see me if you have any problems,' she said. 'I'm always ready to help.'

A few weeks later, Megan wished she had never uttered those words. If the slightest thing went wrong, Jean would call in to her office and regale her with what had happened. The clean towels hadn't been delivered — what should she do? A client had been kept waiting — what should she say to him? Someone had cut their finger badly — should she send them to the hospital? One of the machine operators was making suggestive remarks to the filing clerk — should she reprimand him? What should she do about the driver who had come in late? And so on. Megan tried to be patient and give her the right answers but her own work was suffering as a result of these constant interruptions. Eventually, she went to her manager and asked if someone else could act as coach to Jean as she found it took up too much of her time.

Example 2

Ellis was called into his manager's office and asked if he would like to act as a coach to the new member of staff who was joining them the following month. 'You are a very experienced person,' his manager told him, 'and you're good at listening to people. However, coaching is a skill and I would like you to go on a two-day training course before you start.'

The training course was informative and Ellis felt he had learned a great deal. When the new member of staff joined the team, his manager introduced them, explained that Ellis would be coaching her over the next few weeks until she felt she had settled into the job and knew what she was doing.

Ellis arranged a number of coaching sessions, each about one hour long, explaining that each session would focus on job-related problems that the new member of staff had encountered. 'They are *your* problems,' Ellis was careful to explain, 'so we need to come up with *your* solutions. I'll help you of course, but I want you to think things through for yourself and then come and talk them over with me at the times we've arranged. Of course, if there's a crisis, I'll be around to help as well.'

Over the next few weeks, Ellis and the new member of staff had their pre-arranged meetings and various difficulties with the job were sorted out. Ellis only gave advice when he felt it was absolutely necessary, and he enjoyed seeing her grow in confidence and ability. He also arranged for her to meet some of their customers and talk to them about the kind of after-sales service they expected.

Six weeks later, his manager called Ellis into his office and asked how it was going. Ellis was very enthusiastic. 'It's like seeing a fledgling grow and take its first flight,' he said. 'I reckon she'll be on her own any day now.'

In the first example, neither Megan nor her manager seemed to have much idea what 'coaching' entailed; certainly, neither of them had any training in it. Megan took on all the responsibilities of the new member of staff, which was probably very demotivating for both of them (see Chapter 4 on job satisfaction) and gave the new person no opportunity to seek her own solutions to the problems.

Ellis, in the second example, had the benefit of specialist training and put this into practice. He put aside time in which to see the new member of staff and give her the opportunity to talk to him about what was happening. He also arranged a learning opportunity for her by inviting her to meet customers and hear their point of view. Above all, she learned how to deal with problematic situations herself, and the experience appeared to be mutually satisfying.

Coaching does not need to be restricted to new members of staff. Anyone whose job changes, who needs to learn and apply new skills, or who takes on new responsibilities may benefit from coaching provided that there is someone with experience, time and aptitude to undertake it. As you saw in the first example above, ineffective coaching can have very negative effects.

Coaching style

As with management style (see Chapter 1), there are different styles of coaching, which are appropriate in their turn when dealing with different people or even with the same person in different situations. Evenden and Anderson have identified five styles and the positive and negative effects that each of these styles can have.

- tough   challenges; pushes the other person hard; makes demands; critical

- protective   kindly and reassuring; takes care not to hurt the
                    other person
- calculator   logical; questioning; calm; dispassionate
- whoopee   creative; exciting; everything is fun
- manipulative   provoking; teasing; cajoling

Which of the above styles would you be most likely to use? And
can you see different situations or different people that you might
use them with? More importantly, can you see when and with
whom a style might be inappropriate? Checklist 7.2 demonstrates
when each style can have positive and negative effects on the
coaching relationship.

Checklist 7.2   **Effects of different coaching styles**

Style	Positive effect	Negative effect
Tough	Can push through difficulties when the going is hard.	Can produce rebellion. May lead to bad feeling.
Protective	Can lift up a person when they are low.	Can inhibit development by being over-protective.
Calculator	Can help to find solutions and help the other person to work things out.	Can be seen as impersonal and distant – all head and no heart.
Whoopee	Can motivate by energy and enthusiasm.	Can be seen as frivolous. May avoid tough issues.
Manipulative	Can energise and influence.	May produce anger and feelings of betrayal.

(Evenden and Anderson, 1992)

➡ MENTORING

There is often some confusion about the roles of coaches and mentors, yet it is important that they are seen as having distinctly different responsibilities. A coach, as you have seen, is usually allocated to someone to help them with a particular aspect of their work; this is a short-term situation, finishing when the person being coached has acquired the desired level of performance or skill.

> 'A mentor is someone who guides another individual through important career and life events, encouraging and supporting them, usually because, as mentors, they possess greater experience, knowledge and skill. ... [A] mentor is *not* there to give formal instruction, to try to influence a person's career path unnecessarily, to drag them into company politics or to delegate any of their work to those they are mentoring.' (Thomson and Mabey, 1994)

A mentor can either be allocated or voluntarily selected by the person who requires mentoring, and an individual may have more than one mentor at any one time as the example below illustrates.

Example 3

Ivan is a middle manager in a large public sector organisation. When he first joined the organisation, he was assigned to a manager in another unit, who would act as his mentor. Ivan found the situation difficult since the manager–mentor was a very busy person and Ivan didn't like to disturb him unnecessarily. However, he appreciated the idea of having a mentor and, after a few months, he found another manager who was willing to give him some time to discuss his future.

As he moved up in the organisation, Ivan acquired a number of mentors, people whose judgement he trusted and respected and who were prepared to give up some of their time. One of his mentors was his point of contact for any career-related issues; another, because of her wide organisation knowledge, was always ready to listen to his ideas for improving internal systems, suggesting who he might approach to have those ideas considered formally; another person acted as his mentor when Ivan's partner was seriously ill and Ivan needed to move to part-time working for a while.

Think about the person or people who have acted as a mentor to you, either in a formal or an informal capacity. Checklist 7.3 lists the attributes of an effective mentor – do those people you have thought about match up to the qualities below?

Checklist 7.3 Attributes of an effective mentor

- usually 7–10 years older than the person being mentored
- reasonably senior in the organisation and of higher status than the person being mentored
- has wide and sound knowledge of the organisation
- is interested in the development of others
- is a good communicator
- has an ability to enthuse and motivate others
- commands respect and trust
- is able to give constructive feedback
- is distanced from the day-to-day work of the person being mentored
- has time to invest in mentoring
- is accessible
- is willing to give guidance, information and advice

Obviously, there are many benefits to the individual who is being successfully mentored, including:

- the acquisition of relevant skills and knowledge about the organisation and aspects of the job
- advice on career progression
- increased self-confidence
- increased motivation
- an understanding of the formal and informal processes in the organisation

- an opportunity to discuss aspirations and concerns informally
- clarifying thinking and ideas
- having 'a friend in high places' in the organisation

There are also a number of benefits to the mentor and to the organisation as a whole. The mentor benefits through:

- passing on his or her experience – the satisfaction of sharing knowledge
- increased status in the eyes of peers
- being challenged and sharpening their own thinking

And the organisation benefits through:

- an internal method of informal training
- improved motivation and commitment from staff who are being mentored

However, there are pitfalls in the mentoring relationship. In a formal relationship where a mentor is allocated to one or more people, interpersonal differences may cloud the relationship and make it ineffective. Where mentoring systems have been set up, they require maintaining; they need continued commitment from top management, and mentors need feedback on how they are performing. Turnover of senior staff through retirement, redundancy or leaving for another job can seriously affect a mentoring system very quickly, and there is also the danger that mentors don't keep up-to-date in their particular field. Even when a mentor is chosen voluntarily, the relationship may not meet the expectations of either or both parties. Training for mentors is usually haphazard or non-existent, particularly when the relationship is informal, so that there is a large element of luck involved.

Managers who take on a mentoring role have to be prepared to give time to it and, unfortunately, many organisations do not recognise the time needed to invest in a successful mentoring relationship. In addition, some people feel threatened by younger, high-flying staff and are reluctant to become involved in mentoring.

➡ DELEGATING EFFECTIVELY

Effective delegating is efficient, motivating and developmental. It is not a way of getting rid of the routine and boring parts of your job because, while that may be a more efficient use of your time, it will demotivate the person receiving the work and is unlikely to help in their development. Delegation is the assignment of authority to another person to carry out specific tasks.

The main reasons for delegation are:

- to involve others in decisions and increase their commitment
- to ease the workload of busy managers
- to provide job enrichment
- to increase job satisfaction

Some managers hesitate to delegate authority, being concerned that the job may not be performed to their standard or that they will lose their own authority as a result. Yet the assignment of some degree of authority is essential if delegation is going to work. Robbins (1984) suggests that there are a number of factors that affect how much authority you, as a manager, should delegate, and these are outlined below:

- the size of the organisation – the larger the organisation, the more decisions have to be made and the more tasks undertaken; top managers in large organisations have to rely on delegation to get things done
- the importance of the decision – as you will see in Checklist 7.6, the more important the decision, the less likely it is to be delegated
- task complexity – complex tasks requiring expert or technical knowledge need to be delegated to those who can best perform them

- organisational culture – there needs to be a culture of mutual trust between managers and subordinates to support effective delegation

- quality of subordinates – delegation requires subordinates with the skills and ability to accept delegation

Additionally, there are a number of activities that you have to undertake when delegating in order for the delegation to be successful, as set out in Checklist 7.4.

Checklist 7.4   Activities to undertake when delegating

- Determine exactly what you want to delegate and to whom.

- Clarify the task, or tasks, you want carried out, within a specified timescale and the results you expect.

- Specify how much authority you are assigning with the task, and the limits on that authority – allow your subordinate enough authority to complete the task.

- Discuss the task, its undertaking and completion, and the amount of authority you have assigned with your subordinate, ensuring that the individual understands what is expected and agrees that he or she is happy with the arrangements. Agree how carrying out the task is to be monitored.

- Tell other people that you have delegated the task and authority – this means that others will be aware of the authority vested in your subordinate on this occasion.

Look at the following two examples of delegation and consider why they failed.

Example 4

Joan had been on a course on time management, and one bit of advice that she took to heart was to delegate some of her work to another member of staff so that she could concentrate on the really important issues. She called her assistant, Jan, into her office and explained that she was going to give her more responsibility. 'I want you to take over the weekly returns – you've seen me do them often enough so that will be no problem. Also, I want you to deal with all customer complaints from now on – you can tell me about the really difficult ones in a weekly report, but don't bother me with them at the time. I also want all my phone calls filtered so that only the important ones get through.'

Feeling pleased with herself that she'd given Jan extra responsibility and an opportunity for development, Joan spent the next few weeks concentrating on the launch of a new product and setting up a series of events throughout the country. She was rarely in her office during this time because she needed to inspect the venues and talk to the event organisers in person. When she returned to the office, she was appalled to find a great pile of reports from Jan about complaints from customers, who all expected her to ring them, and other telephone calls she was expected to return although she didn't consider many of them were so important that Jan couldn't have coped with them in her absence. There was also a formal complaint from the Accounts Department about the weekly returns.

Example 5

Lucas knew that the work was getting on top of him and, at his appraisal, his manager had more or less ordered him to delegate some of it. 'You've got that bright trainee in your office – give him a chance to take some of the load off your shoulders.' Lucas spent several days worrying about what he should – and could – delegate. It was all very well for his manager to talk about 'that bright trainee' but Lucas knew only too well what a lot he still had to learn. Eventually, he decided the trainee could cope with some of the more routine jobs, providing Lucas kept an eye on him. He explained at length to the trainee how these jobs should be done and was careful to point out that he, Lucas, retained the authority for them and would be checking up on a regular basis until he was satisfied they were being done properly. But he found checking up almost as time-consuming as doing the jobs himself and the trainee didn't seem to be particularly interested in them anyway.

In the first case, Joan hadn't really thought through which tasks she could delgate to her PA and which ones her PA was capable of taking over. Nor did she brief her on what she considered was 'important' and what she felt the PA could deal with on her own. She didn't give Jan any specific authority to carry out the delegated tasks. In the second case, the reverse happened. Lucas only 'delegated' routine tasks and was constantly checking up to see if they were being performed to his standard. In both cases, the people who were being delegated to would not feel their job satisfaction had increased and, in both cases, the managers ended up with almost as much work to do as before.

Checklist 7.5 outlines some 'dos and don'ts' for a manager to delegate effectively. As you read through them, think about ways in which you currently delegate work to your staff, or ways in which you might do so in the future. Do you think you delegate effectively?

Checklist 7.5   The dos and don'ts of delegation

Do	Don't
Delegate some authority as well as the task.	Delegate too much or too little.
Let the person exercise some initiative.	Delegate responsibility without authority.
Let the person contribute to decisions.	Make all the decisions yourself in advance.
Ensure the person understands what is expected of them.	Give too little information about the task.
Challenge people – explore their potential.	Get rid of dull, routine tasks.
Give constructive feedback.	Delegate and then check frequently.
Offer training when necessary.	Delegate tasks beyond the person's ability.

Delegation can be a very positive developmental opportunity if it is handled properly, but there are problems with it. For example, your staff just may not have the skills and abilities needed to perform some of the tasks you would like to delegate; or you may find that taking time to explain the task to someone is more wasteful than doing the job yourself. Inviting staff to participate in decision making can also consume a lot of time, and this is sometimes just not practical. There can also be problems related to the delegation of responsibility and authority. Other people may not recognise, or may resent, the authority you have delegated to a subordinate; or a valued customer might dislike being assigned to another member of your staff to whom you have delegated the job, despite that person's ability.

Checklist 7.6 gives some examples of the kinds of decisions and tasks that can be delegated.

Checklist 7.6   When to delegate decisions

- when it can be reversed relatively easily if necessary
- when there is an interval between the decision and its implementation
- when there are clear criteria to follow
- when the person to whom you delegate is comfortable with making the decision
- when it is a decision that has to be made frequently
- when the commitment resulting from the decision is relatively short-term
- when the impact on others in the organisation is relatively small

➡ CHRIS'S PROBLEM (7)

Chris has already spent the Department's annual training budget and has just learned that two new people are due to join the team in the next few weeks. One is coming from another company and the other is on secondment from another department in the organisation. As there is no money to send them on a training course, Chris has asked you to suggest ways in which they could be trained at little or no cost. What would you suggest?

References

Armstrong M., *A Handbook of Personnel Management Practice*, 4th edn (Kogan Page, London, 1991)

Evenden R. and Anderson G., *Management Skills: Making the Most of People*, (Addison-Wesley, Wokingham, 1992)

Northcote Parkinson C., *In-Laws and Outlaws* (1959) Chap 4

Robbins S. P., *Management*, 3rd edn, (Prentice-Hall International Inc., 1984)

Thomson R. and Mabey C., *Developing Human Resources* (Butterworth Heinemann, Oxford, 1994)

Chapter 8
Making teams work

'Middle managers often see shop-floor teams as a threat to their authority, and perhaps to their livelihoods; many workers see teams as a source of division and a goad to overwork.'

(*The Economist*, 1988)

Nowadays, everyone seems to think that teams and teamworking are 'a good thing'. And in many cases, this is true. But there are problems, and the generalised middle manager identified in the quotation above seems to be one of them. In their 1993 book *Business without Bosses*, Charles Manz and Henry Sims devote a whole chapter to 'Overcoming the Middle Management Brick Wall', and I shall return to this issue later in this chapter.

Teams serve a number of purposes in organisations and Handy (1985) has identified the main purposes, largely as set out in Checklist 8.1. As you read through the checklist, think about teams or workgroups in your organisation and what functions they fulfil.

Checklist 8.1   The functions of teams in organisations

- distributing, managing and undertaking specific tasks
- problem solving and making decisions
- enabling people to take part in decision making
- co-ordinating and liaising
- passing on information
- negotiating or resolving conflict
- carrying out an inquest or inquiry into the past
- increasing commitment and involvement

  (adapted from Handy, 1985)

In the workplace, you are likely to come across teams – usually defined as formal, work-related groupings of individuals – and groups, both formal and informal. For example, in your organisation you might come across one or more of the following:

- project team
- task force
- committee
- working group
- sports team
- lunch club
- Heads of Department group
- maintenance team
- buzz group
- construction crew
- training team

Some groups are so informal that they don't have a title. These may be groups of people with similar interests, or who work together, and who spend some of their free time with each other during lunch and coffee breaks, travelling to or from work, shopping, or going to the pub. You might refer to these people as your colleagues or workmates, even as your friends at work.

➡ PUTTING ON THE PRESSURE

A number of studies have been carried out on the way people behave in groups – for they do behave differently from the ways in which they behave as individuals. For example, Solomon Asch (1955) describes experiments on the effects of group pressure on individuals. A group of seven to nine people are asked to perform a simple task – to say which pair of lines on two cards are of the same length. Only one member of the group appears to give a different answer from the rest. In 75% of cases, this person would eventually change his or her mind and conform with the group decision. However, the group decision was erroneous as the other members of the group had been instructed beforehand that they should all give the same, wrong answer. Only one individual – the one who did not agree – had not been so instructed. That person, in the majority of cases, had changed his answer because the pressure of six or seven other people had convinced him that he must be wrong. What kind of implication do you think this has for group decision making?

Clearly, this was an experiment and the other members of the group had been instructed to give a wrong answer; this is not how teams behave. Or do they sometimes behave in this way? There may be a reason why a majority of a team's members want a decision to go one way rather than another, and they may bring pressure on other team members to agree with them – even if they are wrong.

People like being in groups. It fulfils part of the social needs we looked at in Chapter 4. Think of all the groups outside work to which people choose to belong – clubs, societies, interest groups, pressure groups and so on. Being with other people who share your interests or goals reinforces your own beliefs and values. Which is why part of creating a successful team involves ensuring all the team members share the same team objectives and are working towards these.

Groups also have 'norms' – that is, a code of acceptable behaviour. They may, for example, have a 'norm' of good timekeeping, so that latecomers are frowned upon; they may, even unconsciously, have a dress code so that if someone turns up in a very formal outfit, he or she might feel uncomfortable if everyone else was casually dressed. When new members join the group, there will be pressure on them, however covert, to conform to the norms of the group. Sometimes, these norms can be negative in effect, as when members of a work group tacitly agree their level of productivity and anyone who exceeds this is reproved.

Another area in which groups can become counter-productive is that of 'groupthink' (Janis, 1972). The group or team becomes so convinced that it is always right that its members ignore or manipulate information or evidence that might suggest that what they are doing or planning is wrong. Groupthink commonly arises when group members are motivated towards being too supportive of the ideas of other members or the group's leader: rather than challenge any apparently questionable decisions or ideas, they strive to maintain what Janis terms '... the cozy, "we-feeling" atmosphere'.

Group pressures are strong because most individuals want to remain as a member of a group to which they belong and hesitate to challenge the group's collective thoughts or beliefs – the result might be ostracism or expulsion.

➡ BUILDING EFFECTIVE TEAMS

Based on work with management students and case studies in industry, Dr Meredith Belbin has written a great deal on teams and teamwork, including the identification of a typology of team roles. This typology helps us to understand why some teams are more effective than others. He also identified some of the attributes of 'winning teams', as follows:

- the attributes of the person in the Chair
- one very creative and clever team member
- a spread of mental abilities and personal attributes in other team members
- team-roles and jobs that match individual attributes of members
- an awareness of team role theory and a recognition of imbalance in roles

Belbin talks of 'the Chair' where we might prefer to use the term 'teamleader'. In Belbin's view, this person should be '... a patient but commanding figure who generated trust and who looked for and knew how to use ability'. However, teamleaders are often chosen for other qualities, such as their proven leadership of other work teams, their technical expertise, their status in the organisation, their knowledge of the organisation etc. In some projects, team leadership will change, depending on the stage of the task. Where, for example, technical expertise is required, the technical expert may well take over leading the team during that phase. In some cases, teams elect leaders from amongst their own members; in others, self-managed teams are set up where all decisions are a group responsibility and there is no team leader.

There are several determinants of group – and team – effectiveness, including:

- size of the group
- the skills and attributes of individual team members
- the task the group is expected to undertake
- the amount of resources and support provided
- external recognition
- leadership style
- group interaction patterns
- motivation and rewards
- stages of group development

and I shall discuss each of these in detail below.

Group size

A large group of around 12 people is likely to have a greater range of skills than a small one of around 4. However, the optimum size of any group will depend largely on the task it is expected to undertake, with a more complex task likely to require more people. Research has shown that people interact less in large groups – there just isn't the time or opportunity. For full participation of all members, the ideal group size is between 5 and 7, and larger groups can be split down into subgroups of this size.

The skills and attributes of individual members

You will recall Belbin suggested that every team needed a very creative and clever person in it. But he would also argue that, if everyone in the team was very creative and clever, it is likely that nothing would ever be achieved; team members would be too busy arguing with each other about their ideas. So all groups and teams need a spread of abilities, as Belbin identifies – people who can take over leadership, analyse, challenge, keep the peace, put forward a logical argument, tie up loose ends, keep records, ensure tasks are carried out and so on. Recognising that effective teams need this range of attributes and skills, and that in some cases there are essential skills missing in the team, is a very important factor in group effectiveness.

The task the group is expected to undertake

I have already mentioned that the task is likely to have an effect on group size; it will also have an effect on team membership because certain areas of expertise may be required for specific tasks. However, the nature of the task is also important; it should be challenging but not impossible and it should be clarified as much as possible so that all group members understand what it is they are expected to achieve.

The amount of resources and support provided

In order to carry out a task, a team will need resources and support in the form of equipment, space, finance or people; the team will need somewhere to meet, and someone to keep notes of meetings and disseminate these; it may need equipment to carry out one or more parts of its task – machinery, plant or computers, for example – and it may need a budget for supplies or other expenditure. Without adequate resources and support, a team is likely to lose its momentum and morale, feeling frustrated that it cannot achieve its objectives.

External recognition

People as individuals and people in groups need to feel that what they are doing is worthwhile and that it is valued by the organisation. Tangible recognition, such as publication of the team's work and results in the organisation's newsletter or on its noticeboard, are ways in which their work can be communicated to a wider audience.

Leadership style

As I have already said, team leaders can change or be non-existent, but many teams still have leaders, often of managerial status. The leadership style needs to be appropriate to the style of the other team members and the task; it would not be very productive to adopt an autocratic leadership style with a team that has been assigned a creative task, for example. However, like everyone else in organisations, teams should have objectives and timescales that need to be met, and the leader's task is often one of monitoring progress and making any necessary adjustments.

Group interaction patterns

This relates to how members of the team communicate with each other and with whoever is their leader. This may be through regular team meetings and team reviews or through less formal interactions, which can sometimes lead to people feeling left out of the communication system. Again, the task will to some extent dictate the best interaction pattern: for a task which needs to be completed quickly and relatively mechanically, the team leader can take most of the responsibility for ensuring everyone knows what they are expected to do; for a more complex, open-ended task, team meetings are a better method of interaction.

Motivation and rewards

This is a complex area since, as you know, different aspects of work motivate different individuals and they also value different rewards (see Chapter 4). As with individual motivation, teams need to know what outcomes and rewards will be provided for effort. They also need to know how they are doing and to receive feedback on performance that can be compared with expectations. Teams, in particular, need to be involved in decisions about their work or that affect the group in any way. Most importantly, the team needs to have a common goal and to be clear what this is.

➡ STAGES OF GROUP DEVELOPMENT

One of the best-known models of the way in which groups behave and develop is that of Tuckman (1965), who identified four stages of group development:

- forming
- storming
- norming
- performing

Each of these stages is outlined in detail below. In each case, I have noted some implications for a team leader of a group going through the various stages.

Forming

This is the initial stage of group formation, when the team comes together for the first time in a new situation. Some of its members may know each other from previous work situations; others may know no one. People behave cautiously towards one another, gauging reactions and usually trying to ensure they make a good first impression. Some people are likely to feel apprehensive at this stage, asking themselves questions such as 'How will I fit in?', 'Can I do the job they expect?', 'How do I stop making a fool of myself?' and 'What's it going to be like?'

As a team leader, you may feel equally apprehensive – after all, the way the team sets about and completes the task will reflect on you personally. It is essential that you are well prepared for this first team meeting since you, too, have to make a good first impression. If possible, you should have been in touch with team members beforehand, at least in writing, explaining who you are to those who don't know you and outlining what you will be doing at the first and subsequent team meetings. However, remember to leave plenty of opportunities for the team as a whole to contribute to deciding how they will work so that they feel they are truly participating in decisions that affect them.

You might take part of the first team meeting to let everyone introduce themselves, giving a brief outline of their experience and specialist expertise. Try to keep this low-key, friendly and relaxed, setting an atmosphere where trust and collegiality can flourish. During this time, there is likely to be heavier dependency on the team leader than in subsequent stages.

The team may take several days, weeks or even months to move out of the forming phase, depending on how often they interact. So, as team leader, you need to be aware of the rate of progress.

Storming

Not all groups go through the storming phase but you will probably find that some individuals in the team will experience this. As the word 'storming' suggests, this is a phase involving conflict. During the forming stage, people usually keep quiet about their own ideas, concerned that they may be challenged or sound foolish. As the team works together, however, individual goals or agendas may emerge and people may feel unhappy about the role they are expected to play in the team. Typical storming behaviour can include:

- sarcasm
- latent or overt hostility towards one or more members of the group, the way the work is being carried out, or the purpose of the task
- challenging of other people's ideas or decisions
- jokes at other members' expense
- confrontational behaviour
- negative comments or behaviour

These behaviours may be directed to one or more individual group members, towards the team leader, or towards the way that the work is being carried out and the purpose of the task. The important thing is to recognise that this is a natural, testing-out stage of team formation and to try to cope with and diffuse the hostility as best you can. This may involve spending time with the individuals concerned to see if differences can be reconciled, listening to their concerns and points of view, and/or encouraging them to seek ways of reaching some kind of agreement. As a leader, you may well feel you are being challenged – and this is likely to be true, for it's all part of the testing-out phase. Try to remain calm; don't allow yourself to enter into conflict actively; try to be flexible and accept that you may in fact be wrong! You could also try to enlist the support of those members of the group who are unaffected – personally – by the storming phase.

Norming

As a team leader, it will be with a sense of relief that you reach this stage – and remember, the 'storming' phase may never occur – where the team begins to work together and group cohesiveness is achieved. The team will establish the ways in which it will work and group 'norms' (see above) will begin to be apparent – a team identity may begin to emerge. This is because team members are beginning to *want* to belong to the team, and so they will give positive support to it. You will need to build on this, sensitively and with care, as you might nurture a young plant that seems to be growing healthily; it could still wither or die if conditions change.

Performing

No group reaches the final stage without having passed through at least two of the earlier ones. This is when the team becomes fully operational and productive, committed to the task and its completion. This is when you become, if not superfluous, at least a background figure, since over-zealous intervention or supervision is likely to be resented.

This is the aspect of team leadership that the managers referred to in the opening quotation and paragraph of this chapter found difficult to cope with. Some managers/team leaders find it hard to withdraw from their position, feeling their status is threatened. By virtually handing over most of the authority for day-to-day decisions to team members, they feel their position as a manager or leader is vulnerable; they believe that their subordinates cannot be capable of the work, for if they are, their own role is endangered.

More enlightened managers may well pass through this stage but then move on to consider the positive aspects of giving the team more responsibility. First, the team is likely to peform well since it is probable that their motivational level is high, and this will reflect well on their erstwhile leader. Secondly, a new role for the manager may well have emerged, namely that of 'the resource'; in this role, the manager is seen as a resource for the team, to call upon as needed, available to give advice, provide information or represent the team's interests to senior management or other parts of the organisation. This role creates its own status and provided an opportunity for managerial self-development.

➡ JOB SATISFACTION AND MOTIVATION FOR TEAMS

You will remember from Chapter 4 that Herzberg identified

- achievement
- recognition
- the nature of the work itself
- responsibility
- advancement

as the five factors most likely to affect job satisfaction in individuals; the same is true of teams. As a team leader, you need to ensure that these factors are accessible to team members and that, as advised in the final stage of group development, they are given as much responsibility over their work as possible.

I have already mentioned the need to ensure team members are clear about outcomes and rewards to be expected from performing well. We can also at this point look again at Maslow's needs-oriented theory of motivation and ways in which you can try to satisfy the team's needs. Checklist 8.2 outlines some ways in which team members' needs can be met. As you read through the checklist, think of a team to which you belong, either as a member or as a leader, and consider ways in which the team's needs might be met more effectively.

Checklist 8.2 Meeting the needs of team members

Physiological needs

- Working conditions are well ventilated and heated/cooled.
- Rest periods are adhered to.
- Furniture is comfortable and ergonomically appropriate for its use.
- Equipment is safe in operation.
- Refreshments are available when needed.

Safety needs

- The team knows what to expect and the outcomes and rewards available.
- You listen to and allay their concerns as much as possible.
- You encourage a working atmosphere of mutual trust and support.
- You provide training for those whose skills need to be improved.
- You give feedback on performance.

Social needs

- Encourage the team to include all its members in its activities.
- Encourage team identity.
- Foster an atmosphere of friendliness.

Esteem needs

- Provide recognition for achievement.
- Respect the views and ideas of others.
- Acknowledge all contributions, however small.
- Diffuse confrontational or conflictual behaviour designed to humiliate others.

Self-actualisation needs

- Aim to motivate team members.
- Ensure the task is suitably challenging.
- Provide opportunities for creativity in decision making and idea generation.
- Reward initiative.
- Foster independence and autonomy

(adopted from Evenden and Andersen, 1992)

➡ WHAT CAN GO WRONG WITH TEAMS

Even when managers and team leaders strive to make teams effective, things can still go wrong. I have already described the dangers of 'groupthink'; in addition, there can be strong interpersonal disagreements and conflicts involving individual team members as well as conflicts between group and individual objectives. Look at the two examples below and think about what you might have done in the team leader's place.

Example 1

Darryl and Cas were both members of a newly-formed project team that had been working together for several weeks. Both carried out their allotted tasks satisfactorily and contributed to team meetings and decisions. But it was obvious to everyone else in the team that they disliked each other intensely. At first, the team leader, familiar with theories of group dynamics, put the behaviour down to group development; she expected it to improve as the team became more immersed in its work. Instead, the conflict became worse. Before, Darryl and Cas had restrained themselves to verbal abuse of each other but now they appeared to be locked into a destructive working pattern where each tried to hinder the other's progress as much as possible. Darryl would, apparently casually, cover Cas's papers with his own drawings and remove the whole pile, leaving Cas searching for the missing documents. In retaliation – or so it seemed – Cas had spilled a mug of tea over a new set of graphics, irreparably smudging them so that Darryl had to start all over again. Not only did their behaviour seem childish and irresponsible, but it was also beginning to affect the overall performance of the team.

Example 2

Emma had been asked to join a working group to look into the feasibility of homeworking for some categories of staff. This was a high-profile group in the organisation and she was delighted at her inclusion. Very soon, however, other members of the group were becoming irritated at her high-handed manner and the way she would try to influence decisions to go the way she wanted. The group leader was surprised; he had heard that Emma was very bright, hard-working and got on well with her colleagues, which is why he had asked her to join the group. But even he began to think she was trying to take over his job when she began setting up sub-group meetings without his knowledge and presenting results as a *fait accompli*.

In the first example, the team leader made enquiries to other team leaders who had Darryl or Cas in their groups. Apparently, providing they were not in the same group, they both worked well as individuals. But their conflict went back a long way and repeated attempts to reduce it had always failed. The only recourse would seem to be to ensure they didn't work on the same team.

In the second case, the group leader eventually called Emma to see him and asked her why she seemed so determined to get her own way, explaining that it was beginning to affect other members of the group. After some probing, she admitted that she saw this project as an opportunity for the promotion she wanted. She had little real interest in the task or in the group's objectives. By taking as much responsibility for decisions as possible, she expected this to count towards her expected promotion. In short, Emma's objectives were quite different from the team objectives.

What these examples show is the negative way in which the behaviour of individuals can affect the performance of the group or of others in general. Early recognition and sensitive handling of interpersonal conflict or inappropriate behaviour can help to avoid more serious problems developing. Unfortunately it is often easier for a team leader to ignore the problem and hope it will go away than to face up to coping with it in its early stages.

➡ THE VIRTUAL GROUP

A recent development has been the interaction of people in a group who do not usually meet face-to-face. This is usually for geographical reasons in that the members of the group are scattered across the country or even across several countries. Instead of holding meetings, they communicate via electronic mail and/or computer conferences.

Much has been written about the isolation of people in virtual groups, but such an approach is often an inexpensive and practical alternative where expertise from different locations is required. Checklist 8.3 offers some suggestions for trying to build an electronic group into a cohesive, working team.

| Checklist 8.3 | **Supporting a virtual group** |

- appropriate hardware and software
- technical support
- training
- agreed conferencing parameters
- conference management
- sub-conferences creation
- encouragement to give feedback
- evaluation

All participants in a virtual group need to have easy access to the right hardware and software, with technical back-up for when things go wrong. Otherwise, unless they are all technical experts themselves, they are likely to become frustrated with delays, slow transfer times, poor pictures in videoconferencing and other problems with the software or hardware. They also need training, even if they are technical experts.

Training in this case is not only in the operation of the software and hardware – navigating their way around the commands and protocols of whatever system they are using – but also in contributing productively to the conference. Some electronic conferences, via specific software or through the Internet, are basically a series of messages from participants. It can be very time-consuming going through each message, working out what it is in response to and even contributing messages yourself. Someone needs to determine the parameters of the conference and promulgate good practice so that it can be managed successfully. Suggested ways of providing conference parameters might include:

- ensuring everyone provides a brief resume of their experience and expertise – as you would expect to get at an initial team meeting when people introduce themselves
- restricting contributions to one screenful of text
- summarising what it is you are responding to before making your response
- deleting or filing contributions out of the conference after a specific period (for instance one month)

When groups interact via a videoconference, there are different, but equally important parameters. Remember the videocamera is static so that if there are a number of people taking part in one location, they cannot always be easily seen or identified. To improve the quality of a videoconference, you should consider:

- limiting the number of people at any one site to no more than six
- insisting that people identify themselves by name before speaking
- disallowing interruptions while someone else is speaking
- summarising and clarifying frequently the main points from the conference

Managing a computer or videoconference can be a skilled task, particularly in the former situation where there are no non-verbal cues available. As the controller of a computer conference, you do have the right to delete facetious, tasteless or useless contributions – but if you are getting any of these, something has already gone wrong with your conference! You should also collate the ideas from the conference every so often and present these in a summary form so that the group can move forward.

➡ MANAGING EXPERTS

One of the more challenging tasks for a team leader is the management of people who are members of the team by virtue of their specialised knowledge or ability. These people may be technical experts, specialists in a particular field such as marketing, finance or administrative systems, external specialists called in to advise the team on areas such as economic viability, local land rights, pollution, ethics and so on.

Internal experts are often full team members but they have a special role in that no one else can do their job; external experts may only join the team as and when invited in an advisory capacity. In both cases, however, it is important that they understand what the team is trying to achieve, how it is going about it and what timescale it is working in; advice given in a vacuum may be worse than useless. As team leader, it would be your job (unless you felt it was something you might realistically delegate to someone else) to brief external experts and to ensure that internal experts were kept up-to-date with team progress and developments.

One drawback, particularly with technical experts, is their habit of using jargon that few of the rest of us can understand. Diplomatically and sensitively, you would need to ask them to avoid this wherever possible or, where it has to be used, to explain what the jargon words mean. Otherwise, you and your team are likely to be floundering in a sea of misunderstanding and the expert's advice will have been worthless.

Mutual respect is the key phrase in all your dealings with experts – and not only with experts but with all team members. Everyone has some expertise to a greater or lesser extent; the technical expert, for example, might be quite unable to write a management report or to produce a budget or to produce creative ideas, but other team members should be able to provide these complementary skills. Value everyone for their expertise, not just the 'experts'.

➡ CHRIS'S PROBLEM (8)

Chris has been asked to get a team together to work on a particular project over the next ten months. You have enquired who is likely to be selected and Chris replies, 'Obviously Marion because she can take minutes of meetings and things like that – I'll need a good secretary. Then I thought of Don because he gets on with everyone and the last thing I want is bickering and backbiting going on all the time – so I won't have Edwin because he's the original pain in the neck. But I was going to ask Alex – she's a nice calming influence on people when things get tough. Then there's the new trainee, she needs some experience. There's a couple of lads from Sales who could be helpful and old Fenshaw because I'm expected to ask him although goodness knows what he can contribute. Other than that, there's me of course, and you – I was just coming to ask if you'd be interested – and another couple of people my manager says I must have. That's about it I think. The first meeting will be some time next week and I'll give you a ring to let you know where it's being held.'

What advice might you give Chris about selecting people to go on the team and running team meetings?

References

Asch S. E., 'Foundations of Conformity and Obedience', *Scientific American* (1955) Vol 193 No 5

Belbin M., *Management Teams: Why They Succeed or Fail* (Butterworth-Heinemann, Oxford, 1991)

Evenden R. and Anderson G., *Management skills: Making the Most of People* (Addison-Wesley, Wokingham, 1992)

Handy C., *Understanding Organisations* (Penguin, London, 1985)

Janis I. L., *Victims of Groupthink* (Houghton Miffin, 1972)

Manz C. C. and Sims H. P. Jr, *Business without Bosses* (John Wiley and Sons Inc., New York, 1993)

Tuckman B. W., 'Developmental Sequences in Small Groups' in *Psychological Bulletin* (1965) Vol 63 No 6, pp. 384–99

Chapter 9
The right person for the right job

'As a personnel management trainee, I was told the perfect advertisement was the one which drew one reply and that was from the ideal candidate.'

(Sir Len Peach, 1985)

Anyone who has wasted their time sorting through hundreds of unsuitable applications for a job would agree with Sir Len Peach's statement above. When you are involved in recruiting new staff, you are usually looking for the right person for the job – when you should be looking for the right person for the *right* job.

In this chapter, you will be looking at the different components of the recruitment and selection process, but not solely from the point of view of the person doing the recruiting and selecting. Looking at the process from the candidates' viewpoint is a helpful way of identifying where recruitment and selection practices are out of date, ineffective or expensive.

Taking on new staff is a big investment decision, as the following calculation shows. I am indebted to my colleague Jon Billsberry for this illustration.

Let's suppose that you are recruiting for a member of staff whose annual salary will be around £17,000 per annum. From your analysis of staff turnover, you would expect this person to stay in the job for three years, so £17,000 multiplied by 3 comes to £51,000. However, that figure only represents the salary paid to the individual; it doesn't include other staff costs such as training, management time, working space, furniture and equipment, bonuses or increments and, of course, the employer's share of National Insurance. The rule of thumb here is that these costs actually double the amount paid out in salary. So, in making a decision to employ someone at £17,000 per annum, you are actually making a decision worth over £100,000. And, if that employment decision is a poor one, so that the person does not perform the job adequately, your costs will increase even more.

A significant cost, particularly if you work in an organisation with high staff turnover or in a rapidly growing business, is that of the recruitment and selection process. I have already referred to the time-wasting process of sorting through unsuitable applications in an effort to create a short list of suitable candidates; to this can be added the time spent in making a selection decision based on interviewing and other selection methods. If you double your own salary and the salary of others involved in the process as we did in the example above, and work out roughly how much each of you is worth per working hour, and how many hours you would spend on the process, you would soon get an idea of the financial investment that is put into recruiting and selecting people.

➡ THE RIGHT JOB

I stressed at the beginning of this chapter that it wasn't just the right person that the recruitment and selection process should identify; it should also identify that the right person is going into the right job. As you saw in Chapter 4, in order to motivate people to perform well, they need to find the job satisfying as well as to value the outcomes and rewards it brings with it.

The first stage in any recruitment process is to analyse the job vacancy, including the tasks that need to be carried out and the skills needed to perform these tasks.

A job description may already exist but this should be treated with caution: it may have been drawn up some time ago and the job has changed since then; or it may be so vague that it could describe almost any job; or it may be an opportunity to change parts of the job itself and how it is carried out. A fresh analysis of the job in question may therefore be worthwhile.

Checklist 9.1 suggests a number of ways in which a job analysis can be carried out, each of which are described in more detail below. As you read through the checklist, think about ways in which you could analyse your own job.

| Checklist 9.1 | **Analysing jobs** |

- observation
- interviewing the jobholder
- interviewing others affected by the job
- questionnaires
- critical incident analysis
- brainstorming

Observation

This involves watching the current jobholder performing the job and noting what skills he or she uses – and, perhaps, what skills are not being used but that might improve job performance. Observation is time-consuming if it is carried out properly, but it will certainly provide you with a view of the job as it is currently performed. Remember, though, that the way it is being carried out at the moment may not be the optimum way you would like it to be undertaken in the future. Analysis of a job through observation should include the essential tasks that make up the job and the skills needs to perform those tasks adequately.

Interviewing the jobholder

Asking the jobholder about the tasks and skills involved in the job can be a useful analysis technique – but remember it is the view of one person, and of a person who probably considers that he or she carries out the job well. It is, however, an opportunity to ask how the job could be improved in terms of job satisfaction and improved performance: maybe some new equipment could cut down on time or wastage, or the job could be enhanced through greater responsibility for decisions on the part of the jobholder.

Interviewing others affected by the job

By interviewing other people who have some involvement with the job, you can gain valuable perspectives that the jobholder alone may not be aware of. For example, how do clients or customers or suppliers view the job? How do subordinates view their supervisor's job? What do colleagues and workmates think about the way the job is structured and how might it be improved to fit in better with their own jobs?

Questionnaires

So far, I have looked at ways of carrying out a job analysis that involves you as a manager in observation and interviewing. Another method is to use a commercially produced questionnaire or checklist (or you might devise your own) that lists a large number of tasks and skills. The jobholder or others affected by the job are asked to complete the questionnaire by identifying which tasks are involved in its performance and what skills are required. Giving the questionnaire to a number of people will identify what the majority consider to be the major tasks and skills involved, and the completed questionnaires can be used as a basis for interviewing.

Critical incident analysis

This is a more sophisticated method of analysis than those above but it is particularly useful where the jobholder has considerable autonomy over how the job is performed. It involves asking the jobholder and others affected by the job to describe as many 'incidents' as possible that they consider to be critical to their success or failure in performing the job. It is often quite difficult for jobholders or others to think of critical incidents, and they may need some notice if you want to use this task.

Brainstorming

As I said earlier, analysing a job that is about to become vacant is an opportunity to look at the way it is currently designed and to consider ways in which it might be improved. This doesn't only include the elements of job satisfaction discussed in Chapter 4, although these are obviously important, but it should also incorporate consideration of different working practices. For example, looking at how it might be carried out by two part-time employees, or someone working flexible hours or working from home could open the job to potential employees who are currently disadvantaged through a variety of personal or domestic circumstances.

Using a brainstorming technique, preferably with the current jobholder and others who are knowledgeable about the job can be useful in looking at the job in a different way, but these people – and you – will all have preconceived ideas of how the job should be carried out. It would be better to involve one or two people who have no knowledge of the job so that a completely fresh perspective is gained.

Brainstorming has a variety of uses, as do other creative-thinking techniques. It has the advantage of being relatively simple to understand as a process and is usually effective in generating ideas. It can be carried out by one person jotting down ideas, but it is preferable to involve a number of people and increase the number of ideas.

Brainstorming should go through the following stages:

- defining the problem or current situation
- generating possible options
- categorising the options
- evaluating the options
- selecting the best option(s) to solve the problem or change the situation

First, you need to be clear about what you are trying to do. In this case, the situation might be described as 'consideration of ways in which this job could be improved', but you would need to clarify such a statement. 'Improved' in what way – for the jobholder, in terms of performance, in terms of productivity or job satisfaction? As a brainstorming group, you would need to come up with a definition of the situation that everyone understood so that they were all clear about what they were trying to do.

Next comes the stage of generating ideas and options. At this point, all evaluations must be suspended and even the most apparently bizarre suggestions recorded without criticism or discussion. This lets people put forward more creative ideas than they would if they thought others were going to make fun of them or dismiss them altogether.

When the supply of ideas has run out, try to group similar options into categories – these categories should suggest themselves depending on the problem and the options. Categorising ideas does not include dismissing any options at this stage; this occurs when you move on to evaluating them. Some ideas may then have to be dismissed for financial reasons or because they do not appear to be feasible. Finally, you should have a small core of options which appear workable. One of these may be a preferable option, or you may agree that more than one are equally feasible. Hopefully, you may have a really creative option that could improve the job significantly.

➡ JOB DESCRIPTION AND SELECTION CRITERIA

If a job analysis is carried out thoroughly, you should have accumulated quite a bit of data, which can now be used to describe the job accurately in the terms outlined in Checklist 9.2.

Checklist 9.2   Describing the job: items to include

- the title of the job
- the tasks involved
- the skills required
- the performance criteria
- the area of responsibility
- line management (upwards and downwards, as appropriate)
- the working environment
- hours of work and working practices

The job description should contain as much information about the job as possible so that potential candidates can decide whether or not they have the requisite skills to perform it adequately and whether or not they want to work in the kind of environment it describes. This is one way of trying to ensure you don't get applications from unsuitable candidates.

Example 1

Laura replied to an advertisement for a finance clerk and was sent some further particulars, including a very brief job description that read:

'The job involves collecting, processing and disseminating financial information in support of the firm's budget, forecasting and monitoring systems. The job holder is responsible to the Head of Finance.'

The description was so insubstantial that she thought she might as well apply anyway and she was shortlisted for the job. During the interview, she was horrified to learn that the company appeared to exist in the Dark Ages and only the Head of Finance had a (rather ancient) computer; the finance clerks were still using adding machines. 'If I'd known that,' Laura told the interviewer, 'I wouldn't have wasted my time or yours by applying for the job.'

An accurate and comprehensive job description should be used to create the criteria for selection – sometimes called an employee specification since it refers to the characteristics, skills and abilities required in the jobholder. There are two categories of selection criteria.

- essential criteria – the job could not be performed adequately unless these are fulfilled
- desirable criteria – these are desirable in the jobholder, but the job might still be performed adequately if these are not fulfilled

Separating criteria out into those that are essential and those considered desirable should ensure that any candidate who does not meet all the essential criteria would not be capable of performing the job adequately and would not be shortlisted. The selection criteria should be sent to all applicants and, again, should act as a filter to deter unsuitable candidates. Your shortlist should contain only candidates who meet all the essential criteria and your eventual selection decision may be affected by the type and quality of desirable criteria that individual applicants fulfil. Had Laura, in the example above, received a set of essential selection criteria that included 'ability to operate an adding machine', warning bells would probably have sounded at that stage.

➡ REACHING THE RIGHT PEOPLE: RECRUITMENT

So far, all that has been discussed has been preparatory work undertaken prior to the recruitment and selection stages. If this work has been undertaken thoroughly, you are already a long way toward Sir Len Peach's ideal at the start of this chapter.

The next stage is to think about how to reach the kind of people who would fulfil the essential criteria for the job, and there are a number of ways of doing this depending on the level and type of person you wish to attract. Checklist 9.3 lists a range of job advertising outlets which you might like to consider. They include internal outlets as well as those outside the organisation. Think again about your own job and which outlets would be most appropriate to recruit someone into that job.

Checklist 9.3   Job advertising outlets

- local press
- national press
- international press/foreign press/specialist press
- trade journals
- professional journals
- employment agencies
- headhunters
- Job Centres
- noticeboards
- the Internet
- internal electronic mail system

- internal newsletters
- university/college noticeboards

Focused advertising will help to reach the right people. For example, it would be rather pointless to advertise for a packer in a professional management journal. Some organisations have a policy of first advertising internally so as to give internal candidates priority, and only to go outside the organisation if no one suitable is found within it.

The advertisement is not only a method of reaching the right person; it is also a statement about your organisation. For example, it should never contain statements that are discriminatory on the grounds of sex, race or ability and, increasingly, on the grounds of age; this immediately tells readers something about the organisation and its apparent lack of an equal opportunities policy, which could deter potential candidates. A recruitment advertisement can be seen as an opportunity to 'sell' the organisation in statements such as:

- 'Sewandsew plc is the leading European manufacturer of electronic sewing machines.'
- 'Anglican Water is committed to meeting the needs of its customers in the most cost-effective way.'
- 'Flippers Inc has an IiP Award and cares about the people it employs.'

These statements create favourable impressions in the minds of readers, encouraging them to apply for a job in a successful, efficient and/or caring organisation.

Advertisements should not be placed in whatever outlets the organisation chooses until the further particulars are available, so that enquirers can be sent these on request. Further particulars should include the job description and selection criteria as discussed in the last section and, ideally, the name of a person to contact if the applicant wants to ask any questions before deciding whether or not to apply for the job. If the organisation has an application form, this should also be included, and some indication of what you expect in an application should be given.

Example 2

> Colin had decided to apply for another job in the organisation in
> which he was currently working. There was an advertisement that
> interested him on the noticeboard and he sent off a letter applying
> for it. Some time later he got a letter from the Personnel
> Department which confirmed his application. A week later another
> letter came, saying that he had not been shortlisted since his
> application did not include enough information. Colin felt
> aggrieved at this; he had thought that because all his staff records
> were available in the Personnel Department, he didn't need to
> complete a formal application form.

Think about the above example and how the information in the
(internal) job advert could have been improved.

➡ MAKING AN INFORMED CHOICE: SELECTION

Shortlisting

Shortlisting is the first stage in the selection process. Hopefully, if
the preparatory and recruitment stages have been effective, your
choice may be difficult because it is between a small number of
very good candidates, but at least it won't be timewasting. It is
often better to have more than one person involved in shortlisting,
particularly for skilled and senior jobs. If the method of selection is
to be by an interview panel, then everyone on that panel should be
involved in shortlisting.

Shortlisting needs to be done fairly and objectively on the basis
of the essential and desirable criteria; this is not the time to change
those criteria! As you consider which candidates should be called
in to take part in the selection process and those you consider
should be rejected, think about what you are going to say to the
rejected candidates. A brief letter of rejection is not only hurtful, it
could deter that person from applying for jobs in that organisation
again or, if no valid reason for rejection is given, it could initiate a
complaint of discriminatory rejection. Particularly in the case of
internal candidates, someone should be assigned to give personal

feedback to unsuccessful candidates, either at the shortlisting or the selection stage.

Preparing for selection

The shortlisting having been completed and both successful and unsuccessful candidates notified, you are now approaching the final stages of the selection process. Interviews are still the commonest form of selection, mainly because they provide an opportunity for meeting the candidates. They are not (and can never be) truly objective, although they can be structured to provide as much objectivity as possible. The main methods of selection are detailed in Checklist 9.4. As you read through the checklist, identify the methods used in your organisation or those that you have been involved in as a candidate yourself.

Checklist 9.4   Methods of selection

- interviews
- personality tests
- assessment centres
- work simulation
- aptitude tests

Interviews

Selection interviews can be carried out by one person or by several, constituted into one or more interview panels; the panel interview is obviously less subjective than the one-to-one interview since different people will have their own preferences and perspectives. The only way to ensure that an interview is as fair and objective as possible is to stick strictly to the selection criteria when asking questions and, in general, asking the same questions of all candidates. The only time it would be acceptable to vary from this practice is when you are trying to elicit facts that may be missing or unclear in the candidate's application. If you follow a structured interview based on the selection criteria, it is possible to score candidates' responses on a predetermined scale, which can give you as objective an outcome as possible.

Unstructured interviews can be very subjective and unfair; they can also lead to accusations of discrimination if certain questions are asked of some candidates and not others. Although it is illegal to ask questions about the candidate's personal life in respect of childcare provision, marital or partnership relationships, religion and so on, it still happens. The golden rule is only to ask questions that relate to the performance of the job.

One thing to remember is the fatigue factor in interviewing. If your shortlist is, in fact, rather a long list, you would be better to run the interviews over more than one day. Otherwise, trying to cram too many people in to one day will just result in mental paralysis and interviewer exhaustion – which is unfair on the candidates and the panel.

The kinds of questions asked can vary depending on what kind of response you are looking for. Types of questions used in selection interviewing include:

- direct questions – establishing or confirming a fact
- probing questions – eliciting further information
- hypothetical questions – designed to find out what the candidate might do in a hypothetical situation
- reflective questions – asking the candidate to reflect back on something said earlier

Types of questions that should be avoided include:

- discriminatory questions – not asked of all candidates and usually pertaining to the candidate's personal life
- multiple questions – complex questions requiring the candidate to make a series of responses

With panel interviews, the people involved need to agree beforehand who is going to chair the panel and which questions or areas each member of the panel is going to concentrate on. The Chair will be responsible for:

- introducing the panel members to the candidate, with some indication of their role in the organisation
- putting the candidates at their ease before launching into the interview itself
- asking the candidates (at strategic points in the interview, or at the end) whether they have any questions
- bringing the interview to a close
- chairing the post-interview discussion

The Chair needs to ensure that candidates have been told the date and time of their interview and where to attend, as well as after the interview giving them some indication of how and when they will be notified of the panel's decision. The Chair will also need to ensure that all the documentation for the interview is available for panel members, and Checklist 9.5 outlines what this involves.

Checklist 9.5   **Documentation for interviews**

- For each candidate (where appropriate):
  - a completed application form
  - a CV
  - results of any tests the person has carried out before the interview
  - references/details of referees
- the job description
- the selection criteria
- details of any scoring system to be applied when assessing candidates

Personality tests

These are used by organisations where it is believed that you can predict job performance and behaviour from personality characteristics such as sociability, self-confidence, competitiveness, decisiveness and so on. There are a number of valid tests available for assessing these and other personality traits, but most need to be administered and scored by trained psychologists.

Assessment centres

These were discussed earlier in Chapter 6, where we referred to them as development centres when used for assessing skill levels in the context of staff training and development. Here they have a similar use and might include a range of instruments to test intelligence and skills. Assessment centres are costly to run unless they are also used in staff development or when recruiting large numbers of people for similar jobs. Again, they are usually administered by trained psychologists.

Work simulation

These are tests which are used to determine how skilled a person is at one or more aspects of the job. Typically, for example, a secretary may be asked to carry out a piece of work on a word processor, and there are work-related tests for example for book-keeping, operating some types of machines, for caterers, hairdressers and so on. With the advent of National Vocational Qualifications (NVQs) in the last few years, the award of a relevant NVQ can take the place of work simulation since the award testifies to the level and amount of competence an individual has attained in a certain skill area.

Aptitude tests

These are tests of physical and mental ability. For example, if a job involves certain physical skills, it is possible for the candidate to be asked to perform these skills on the job as part of the selection process. Tests of mental ability include assessing levels of literacy, numeracy and intelligence. None of these tests should be used unless they are directly relevant to the performance of the job. For example, someone who is weak numerically may be able to operate a calculator to compensate for this and may not in fact need much in the way of numeracy skills to perform the job.

The main thing to remember with all these selection methods is that you need to choose the one or ones most appropriate and relevant to performance of the job. It may be a good time to look at the recruitment and selection methods used in your organisation at this point. Are they outdated? Do they result in selecting the best person for the job – and the right person for the right job? What other methods might be substituted or improved upon?

Whatever method or methods your organisation uses to select staff, the final decision will have to be made, resulting in one or more successful candidates and probably a greater number of unsuccessful ones. However, some of these may have been very good candidates, which your organisation would like to encourage to re-apply for other jobs in the future. If your recruitment and shortlisting processes were effective, the majority of rejected candidates should fall into this category. Thus, any letter of rejection needs to be carefully worded so as to ensure that rejected candidates understand why they were unsuccessful this time but should consider applying again in the future. Internal candidates should receive some feedback and counselling if they have been unsuccessful.

It is also a useful exercise for the panel to reconvene after the selection process is over to reflect on what happened and consider ways in which they might improve the selection process another time.

➡ APPLYING YOURSELF

So far, we have looked at the recruitment and selection processes from the organisational perspective and from the viewpoint of people in the organisation who are responsible for undertaking these tasks. Now I want to turn the tables and suggest that you think about some of the aspects from the candidates' viewpoint. While not all managers are involved in recruitment and selection of staff, all have been candidates at some time and it is helpful to reflect on that experience.

Looking for a job

If you look back to Checklist 9.3 (Job advertising outlets), the same list could be used when you are looking for a job. Obviously, if you are seeking promotion or a different job within your organisation, you will know about internal vacancies and where to find them. But it is often sensible to discuss your career moves with your appraiser or your mentor so that they may be able to let you know in advance when a vacancy is likely to be coming up. Outside the organisation, the press and journals are the most common sources of job advertisements and you should consider focusing on those publications that seem to carry details of jobs in the category you are seeking.

Read the advertisements with care – it is time-consuming to write off for particulars of a large number of jobs and can be expensive in postage. Check whether they require certain qualifications or skills that you may not possess; if you don't have them, it is likely you will not be shortlisted so why waste everyone's time? If you are in doubt, you might ring the company up and see if they would accept alternative qualifications or provide training in the skills you lack.

Equally, if and when you receive the further particulars and details of how to apply, read these carefully and follow the instructions. I have been on numerous selection panels and registered dismay when seeing partially completed application forms, letters of application when a form has been sent out, and dredged-up CVs that bear no relation to the job that is being advertised. Even if you are applying for a number of jobs, treat each one as if it is the only one available and then you are much more likely to be shortlisted.

The curriculum vitae (CV)

There are a variety of ways in which a CV can be presented – on a skills basis, chronologically, subdivided into sections on education and qualifications, work experience, other experience, skills and so on. All have their advantages and disadvantages. The most important aspect of the CV is that it should be *related to the job for which you are applying* and this means re-creating it for each application. Having a CV created for you by someone else may be a waste of money since it will be generic and not related to any particular job vacancy. Creating a customised CV for each job is not too difficult if you have access to a word-processor, and it may well be worth the time put into it even if you have to start from scratch for each job application.

The easiest way to create a customised CV for each job is to construct a database from which you can draw relevant data. This should ideally be on a computer but it can be equally useful on a cardfile. Checklist 9.6 details headings under which you could file the kinds of data your personal CV database should contain. Using the information sent to you by the prospective employer, pull out the relevant data and match it to the requirements of the job. Use an imaginative layout so that it is concise and easy to read.

Checklist 9.6   The CV database

- personal details (address, contact phone number/fax/e-mail address etc.)
- education (secondary, further, higher)
- qualifications gained
- courses attended
- membership of professional societies
- jobs held (title, organisation, dates of employment)
- responsibilities held
- achievements
- skills
- non-work experience and responsibilities (PTA, councillor, magistrate, youth leader etc.)

References

Most employers will ask for referees and it is essential that you contact your chosen referees before committing them – as it is only courteous to do so. Again, you should choose your referees in relation to the job so that they can provide references that are relevant to the kind of work you want to do. Some employers will ask for a character reference – usually provided by someone of standing in the community such as a priest or vicar, a doctor, schoolteacher or lecturer, magistrate or judge. If the organisation has not done so, an applicant should send referees copies of the job description and selection criteria; a good referee will match their reference to these requirements.

Application forms

If an organisation asks you to complete an application form, you should certainly do so and not send a letter with an attached CV. There is a purpose in application forms as it allows the selectors to compare applications more readily since all are being asked to supply the same information. You can use your CV database here as well, since most application forms ask for details of education and employment history. You should aim to present your application form in a clean and tidy state, so have several practice runs first before you decide to commit words to paper; you might like to photocopy the blank form several times for this purpose. Check your spelling and grammar and ensure that your handwriting is clear.

Covering letter

You should send a covering letter with any application and use this as an opportunity to outline – very briefly – why you think you would be a suitable candidate for the job. Address the letter to a named person if you can, but if no name has been given, you should address it to 'Dear Sir/Madam' (and end 'Yours faithfully'!).

Taking part in the selection process

When you are called for interview, ensure you know where you are going: make a practice journey in advance so that you are quite clear about public transport or car parking arrangements and are not likely to arrive late. Do your homework: find out as much as you can about the organisation. You can get information from other employees, from the data sent to you before you applied, from the library and so on. This will enable you to ask intelligent questions which demonstrate that you are interested in the organisation.

However casual the organisation is, one where all the employees wear jeans and trainers for example, it is still expected that prospective candidates will be dressed formally and present a neat and tidy appearance. But there is also a need to be comfortable; you may have to wait around for some time, especially if you are taking part in a battery of tests as well as an interview, and uncomfortable clothes or shoes will only increase your natural tension at this time.

Try to be relaxed but not too 'laid-back'. You are aiming to give a good first impression because, particularly in interview situations, these impressions still count. Have some questions you want to ask – write these down if you want to and tell the interviewers you need to refer to them. And if you find any of the questioning offensive because, for example, you feel you are being questioned in a certain way because you are a woman, or a member of an ethnic minority group or have a disability, you have every right say so. You may not get the job – but you may not want to work for that kind of organisation anyway.

After the selection process, if you have been unsuccessful, you may want to ring up someone in the organisation who was involved in it and ask for some feedback and why you didn't get the job. This is a learning experience and you should see it as such.

➡ CHRIS'S PROBLEM (9)

Chris has been asked to take on the recruitment and selection of a new supervisor as the existing one is taking early retirement. 'Easy,' says Chris, 'I've asked Harry for the job description and sent an advert out to the local rag. I'm bound to get loads of applications – unemployment is running at an all-time high around here at the moment. Once I've sorted out who to interview, I thought I'd get everyone to do some kind of test or something – they're very popular these days and it would impress my manager. Then I'll run the interviews – 15 minutes should be long enough for each one I reckon. I know Jaswinder is applying for the job and he's the one I want anyway so I'm not going to waste my time over the rest. What do you think?'

What would you say to Chris?

References

Peach, Sir I., *The Times*, 29 August 1985

Chapter 10
Sensitive situations

**'Make every bargain clear and plain
That none may afterward complain'**

(Ray, 1670)

One of the main causes of industrial conflict is misunderstanding. Often this is because senior management or superiors assume that they know best and that it is not necessary to consult with, or even inform, the workforce or subordinates. As a result, rumour and hearsay abound, creating situations that, if left to fester, could escalate into full-scale industrial action. Sometimes this action is entirely justified; sometimes it could be avoided. And by 'industrial action' I don't only mean mass walk-outs or strikes, but the kind of action that can be taken by an individual with a grievance, real or imagined, against the organisation.

Part of the problem lies in communication, as you saw in Chapter 2; the Receivers in this case have misunderstood the messages sent by the Senders. Other causes may lie in a genuine grievance with the way in which the organisation, or some of its members, are conducting themselves.

In this chapter, I shall be setting up a number of scenarios that illustrate the kind of incidents that can occur in the organisational context. As a manager, you may have the opportunity to prevent these incidents causing more serious dissatisfaction, by correcting any misunderstandings that may have arisen or through dealing with the situation at an early enough stage to prevent a full-blown grievance. These are, as the title of the chapter suggests, 'sensitive' situations, often involving people's emotions and heightened feelings of anger, animosity and anxiety. They are the kinds of situations that many managers would prefer to avoid – mainly because most managers have never had any training in how to deal with them, nor any training and experience of counselling upset staff.

➡ RULES AND PROCEDURES

Before looking at examples of situations in the work place, it is essential to recognise the importance attached to procedures concerned with grievance and taking disciplinary action. There is a legal obligation in the UK under the Employment Rights Act 1966 for employers to provide all employees who work more than eight hours a week with:

- the name of the person to whom a grievance may be taken
- the organisation's grievance procedures (or where these can be found)
- the rules governing disciplinary action (or where these can be found)

and these should be contained in the terms and conditions of employment. Because of this, failure by an organisation to deal with an employee's grievance can be seen as being in breach of contract and the employee can claim damages. Making the rules and procedures clear makes good sense. After all, if employees don't know what the organisation considers to be a disciplinary offence, they should not be penalised for committing one.

Grievance procedure

Organisations will vary in the kind of grievance procedure that they expect their employees to follow, but Checklist 10.1 outlines some common stages. As you read through that checklist, think about the grievance procedure in your own organisation. Are all employees aware of it? Are you familiar with it?

Checklist 10.1 **Stages in a grievance procedure**

(1) Verbal report of grievance by an employee or group of employees to their immediate supervisor.

(2) Supervisor responds within three working days.

(3) Written report of grievance by an employee or group of employees to their line manager.

(4) Manager responds within five working days.

(5) Line manager arranges meeting with senior management.

(6) Third-party intervention may be brought in.

(7) Employee has right of appeal.

Of course, not all grievances should, or do, go through all the stages outlined in Checklist 10.1 and it is usually preferable that they do not. There are a number of stages at which settlement of the grievance can be made. The supervisor at Stage 2 may be able to settle a minor grievance which comes under his or her control. Similarly, the line manager can have the responsibility of settling a more serious grievance. It is only when senior management fails to settle the grievance that the intervention of a third pary, such as the Advisory, Conciliation and Arbitration Service (ACAS), may be necessary.

Disciplinary procedure

As we saw earlier in this section, employees need to know what kind of offences can be classified as warranting disciplinary action. Checklist 10.2 outlines some of the commoner causes of disciplinary action.

Checklist 10.2 **Common causes of disciplinary action**

- persistent lateness
- insubordination
- smoking (if the company has a no-smoking policy), drinking alcohol, taking non-prescribed drugs during working hours and/or on company property

- not taking due care of company property and equipment
- causing malicious damage to company property or equipment
- using the company telephone for personal calls
- ignoring Health and Safety rules
- causing harassment to other employees

The checklist is by no means exhaustive and organisations will have additional and different rules for the way they expect their employees to behave depending on the work they are undertaking. For example, employees working with hazardous substances or machinery will be expected to obey a strict set of rules governing health and safety in the working environment. A secretary in an office would not be expected to follow the same rules, but there would still be health and safety issues to be observed in that office, such as taking breaks from working at a VDU and avoiding dangerous cables from computers and telephones.

Some of the causes of disciplinary action need to be detailed more clearly than in the checklist. For example, how does the organisation define 'persistent' lateness? And when does genuine questioning of instructions become 'insubordination'? How does the organisation view 'due care' of property and equipment and when is accidental damage acceptable? Unless employees are clear about when their behaviour is classified as breaking organisational rules, they may unwittingly transgress.

As with the grievance procedure above, taking disciplinary action against an employee goes through a number of formal stages and Checklist 10.3 below outlines these. Again, as you read through the checklist, ask yourself if all your staff are aware of the organisation's rules and of the procedure for taking disciplinary action.

Checklist 10.3   **The stages in a disciplinary procedure**

(1) Interview with supervisor or line manger.

(2) Supervisor/line manager issues verbal warning.

(3) Supervisor/line manager records outcome of interview.

(4) Second interview with supervisor/line manager.

(5) Supervisor/line manager issues first written warning.

(6) Third interview with supervisor/line manager.

(7) Supervisor/line manager issues final written warning.

(8) Disciplinary action (e.g. suspension, dismissal) is carried out.

(9) Employee has right of appeal.

As with Checklist 10.1, it is to be hoped that few cases go through all the stages of the procedure and that disciplinary proceedings can be ended at one of the early stages.

Investigating grievance complaints and cases of alleged misconduct

As a manager, you will probably be involved in carrying out initial investigations into the cause of a complaint made by an employee or brought against an employee. This means concentrating on the facts and gathering evidence in support of those facts. Evidence may be gathered from the person making the complaint and from witnesses to an incident – for example, people who have overheard an employee making remarks that could be construed as sexist or racist. Only when you have collected as much factual evidence as possible can you make a decision as to how to proceed. The evidence should be recorded in writing where possible since it will form part of the written record of the next stages.

At every stage in the investigation of a grievance or a disciplinary offence, written records are essential. They become particularly important if the case escalates and the employee appeals against the outcome. These written records should be copied to the employee and also placed on his or her personal file. Records of relatively minor offences such as lateness are usually kept on this file for 12 months providing there have been no more instances of that offence. For more serious offences, such as an unprovoked attack on another employee, the expiry period is usually lengthened to two years.

➡ COPING WITH POTENTIAL GRIEVANCE AND DISCIPLINARY SITUATIONS

Set out below are a number of scenarios that you might expect to encounter as a manager. As you read through them, think about how you might cope with them if a similar situation cropped up in your own department.

Example 1

Candice had come to the UK from America and applied to join the police force in London. She was sent on the initial training course and, after a few days, her instructor reprimanded her for wearing too much make-up and, in particular, for wearing a brightly coloured lipstick. Candice was upset about this; she could not see how wearing make-up detracted from her performance as a policewoman. She received two further warnings about wearing make-up but continued to do so and was eventually dismissed.

Example 2

Andy was normally a quiet, self-effacing individual who carried out his work as a porter in a large hospital efficiently and carefully. One afternoon, another porter came into the supervisor's office, holding a cloth over his nose which appeared to be bleeding profusely, claiming that Andy had attacked him with a broom handle for no reason at all. Knowing the second porter to be a habitual trouble-maker, the supervisor refused to believe his story of an unprovoked attack and insisted that he must have said or done something quite serious to have made Andy behave in that way. The second porter made a formal claim of grievance against Andy and against the supervisor.

Example 3

Julius had been coming in late for work on two or three days a week for a month and his supervisor had asked his manager to have a word with him. 'Nothing I say seems to make any difference,' complained the supervisor. 'He'll be all right for a day or two and then it starts up again.' The manager called Julius in to see him and asked him why he was coming in late, but Julius just shrugged and said he had 'problems at home'. The manager carefully explained that he was breaking the rules by not coming in on time and that his lateness was having an effect on others in the section. He was to consider this as a verbal warning and the first stage in a disciplinary procedure.

Example 4

Sol had managed for the third time to break the spindle on one of the most expensive pieces of equipment in the factory. His supervisor was furious. 'You're just careless and thoughtless,' he raged at Sol. 'Now that machine will be out of action for a couple of days while a new spindle is fitted, losing us time and money. I'm giving you a verbal warning that if this happens again, I'll start taking disciplinary action against you.' Sol looked surprised. 'Why?', he asked. 'It was an accident. Just shows the machine isn't up to much if you ask me. You can't make a disciplinary case out of an accident or faulty machinery.'

Example 5

Arnold was not a particularly good or reliable worker and when he missed the night shift he was due to work immediately before going on holiday, his supervisor saw this as an opportunity to get rid of him. He followed the organisation's disciplinary procedures and Arnold was dismissed.

Example 6

Margo had worked for the council for 23 years when she was dismissed for clocking another employee's card. She maintained that she had only done this because the other employee, a long-time friend of hers, had forgotten her purse and gone back to look for it. Margo insisted she had only been doing her friend a good turn and that both of them had arrived at work at the same time. But the council's handbook for employees clearly stated that falsification of clockcards would result in instant dismissal, and an industrial tribunal upheld the penalty.

In the first case, a lot would depend on whether the rules of the police force explicitly forbade the wearing of make-up during training. If they did, then Candice was clearly in breach of a written rule, although it would also have to be established that she had been given a copy of the rules or told where she could obtain them. Not having read the rules if she had access to them would not be accepted as an excuse. However, if there was no rule governing the wearing of make-up during training, or Candice had not been given, or told where to obtain, the rules, she would have a case for appeal. As a manager, these are the kinds of facts you would need to establish before going on to any further stages of disciplinary action.

In the second case, the supervisor was clearly at fault in letting his knowledge of the two men cloud his initial judgement. Even though he thought it unlikely that Andy would make an unprovoked attack, he should have established the facts, preferably involving any witnesses. It would be likely that the porter could claim breach of his employment contract because the supervisor had refused to listen to his complaint.

The case of Julius could well be a complex one. In the first place, it would appear that neither the supervisor nor the manager had made much effort at finding out what the 'problems at home' involved. Problems outside the workplace might be considered to be outside the responsibility of the supervisor or the manager and, probably in 'the letter of the law', this would be true. But as I have been pointing out in this book, managers have a responsibility for managing people – and people's lives and concerns do not necessarily divide neatly into 'home' and 'work'. One approach might have been for the manager to encourage Julius to talk about his problems and discuss how they might be solved in relation to his persistent lateness, thus avoiding taking disciplinary action.

Again, the case of Sol could be seen as having been insensitively handled. Maybe Sol was right and the equipment was faulty. It would be difficult to prove that he was breaking the spindle deliberately unless there were witnesses to the incident. The supervisor should not have lost his temper but should have considered ways in which these recurring 'accidents' could be prevented or ways in which it could be proved that the breakage was either accidental or deliberate.

The case of Arnold is based on a real-life incident and Arnold appealed against the dismissal. His appeal was upheld because, in the company handbook, the penalty for taking extra leave before a holiday was not specifically stated so the employee was not aware of it (Owen, 1995). The supervisor saw the incident as the excuse for getting rid of a low-performing employee.

In the last case, the reverse was true because the penalty for falsification of clockcards was clearly stated in the council's handbook for employees. Despite Margo's long service and her avowed motive of helping her friend, the organisation had every right to dismiss her. For one thing, there was only her word (perhaps supported by someone who was her close friend) that she had falsified the clockcard only once and for the reason given. Had the organisation turned a blind eye to this breach, there would have been a precedent set for other employees to falsify each other's cards.

➡ PROBLEMS IN THE WORKPLACE

Harassment

One of the difficulties about establishing whether harassment is taking place is that it has to be defined as 'unacceptable behaviour', and 'unacceptable' is further defined as 'unwanted, unreasonable and offensive' by the European Union. What may be unacceptable to one person may be acceptable to another – or, at least, tolerated by others.

Herein lies a dilemma. Should all employees 'blow the whistle' on someone whose behaviour is considered to be unacceptable by the minority, whereas the majority find the behaviour acceptable? If you are one of the minority, for example a woman in a predominantly male workplace or someone from an ethnic minority group, you may find it difficult to convince others that behaviour you consider to be harassment is unacceptable to you and should be stopped. And, not all women, nor all members of an ethnic minority group may agree on what is unacceptable behaviour towards them. However, harassment is a very real issue in the workplace and is not confined to minority groups, as you can see from the examples below.

Example 7

Dale went to his manager complaining of harassing behaviour from a group of his colleagues. He had recently left his wife after a long and unhappy marriage and was now living with another woman whose marriage had broken up a few years earlier. Several of his workmates felt he had behaved badly by leaving his wife, although none of them knew the full story. He claimed he was being ostracised and had been sent anonymous letters accusing him of adultery. This attitude from his workmates was affecting his health and he was now taking sedatives on the advice of his doctor.

Example 8

Tracy had been absent from work on several occasions, claiming some mystery illness, but she had not been to see a doctor about it. When her manager questioned her about this, she became upset and said that everyone was against her because she did extra work for one of the directors. Apparently, the director had singled her out because of her quick and accurate word processing, and when his own Personal Assistant was too busy, he asked Tracy to undertake the extra work. At first, she had been pleased to do this but it had soon started to create problems for her in the office. The other secretaries made sneering remarks about favouritism and 'crawling to the boss'; her desk had been rifled and her possessions left all over the floor; on several occasions, work she had finished had unaccountably vanished and she had had to do it again. She had started to stay at home on certain days so that the director would stop asking her to do work for him.

Example 9

Bill was highly embarrassed when he eventually came to see his manager. Apparently a homosexual member of his work group had started to make sexual advances to him, which Bill found distasteful and humiliating. His other workmates told him to treat it as a joke, and that he should not cause trouble for the other man by making a complaint. But Bill found it was affecting his work and his concentration and he felt his relationships with all the members of the group were suffering.

Harrassment is unacceptable if it is behaviour that another individual finds:

- unwanted
- unreasonable
- offensive
- humiliating
- intimidating
- hostile.

It can be combated in a number of ways, as Checklist 10.4 demonstrates. As you read through the checklist, think about measures in your own organisation that already exist, or that could be put in place, to combat harassment.

Checklist 10.4 Combating harassment at work

- Ensure there is a published equal opportunities policy.
- Treat all complaints of harassment seriously.
- Take action against complaints.
- Ensure that harassment is identified as gross misconduct in the organisation's disciplinary procedures and that, if proven, it will lead to dismissal.
- Make sure that anyone complaining of harassment can circumvent the grievance procedure and go straight to senior management, or put in place a separate procedure to deal exclusively with cases of harassment.
- Appoint and train counsellors who can assist those being harassed.
- Train those who play a part in the resolution of complaints.

(adapted from *Sexual Harassment in the Workplace*)

Bullying and violence

While harassment usually takes a verbal form, physical bullying and violence is equally to be abhorred. Bullying is now recognised as a major contributor to stress and stress-related illnesses at work and may consist of threats of physical violence or disturbance rather than actual assault. It is usually an expression of power from someone in a more senior position or from someone who is physically bigger and stronger than his or her victim. Although bullying can be construed as intimidation, the employee does not have the automatic right to make a claim to an industrial tribunal as is the case in situations of sexual or racial harassment. As a result, much workplace bullying goes undiscovered until it is too late and the victim's health is affected or he or she leaves the organisation. The two examples below illustrate the inequity of workplace bullying.

Example 10

Everyone knew Denise was a bully. She had been made a project manager a few years earlier and the power she gained as a result went straight to her head. If you questioned her decisions, or criticised her in any way, she had ways of making you realise your mistake. Alex had tried to stand up to her. He felt she was making everyone's life difficult and all she wanted was for everyone to agree with her ideas and tell her she was wonderful. At a team meeting, he challenged her decision to reorganise two of the subgroups, telling her they were working well as they were and to reform them would just cause problems. After the meeting, Denise called him into her office and told him he would never get promotion in this department while she was manager. Moreover, she was going to report him for insubordination. Alex realised that she was quite capable of carrying out her threats *and* that it would be very difficult for him ever to prove she had made these statements.

Example 11

Tim was new to the section and had only joined the company a year earlier. For some time he suffered taunts about his lack of stature and his weak arm, neither of which prevented him from doing the job. At last he lost his temper with one of the older men and threatened to report him for harassment, but the man just laughed. 'You do that, son,' he was told, 'and you won't just have one weak arm, you'll be lucky to walk straight again. And what's more, no one will take your part against me.'

Actual physical violence is defined by the Health and Safety Executive as: 'Any incident in which an employee is abused, threatened or assaulted by a member of the public in circumstances arising out of the course of his or her employment.' In fact the bullying of Tim in the last example could come under this heading but, as Tim knew only too well, it would be very difficult to prove. Checklist 10.5 outlines the reasons why both employers and employees should have an interest in reducing violence in the workplace.

Checklist 10.5 **Why violence in the workplace should be reduced**

For the employer, violence can:

- lead to low morale
- create a poor image for the organisation
- make it difficult to recruit staff
- make it difficult to retain staff
- increase absenteeism
- raise insurance premiums and compensation payments

For the employee, violence can:

- cause pain and suffering
- result in disability or death
- create anxiety and stress

The Health and Safety Executive have suggested a seven-step programme in which employers and employees work together to reduce workplace violence and violence to staff from encounters with members of the public.

Step 1: establish that there is a problem through observation and by listening to the comments of employees and others.

Step 2: record all incidents to help to establish the size and severity of the problem.

Step 3: classify all incidents – examples are given below.

Type of incident	Results
Involving physical contact.	Fatal injury; major injury; injury or emotional shock requiring first aid; out-patient treatment; counselling; absence from work (record the number of days).
Involving serious or persistent threats or verbal abuse.	Emotional shock requiring counselling or absence from work (record the number of days); feeling of being at risk or under great stress.

Step 4: decide on preventive measures to reduce violence to staff from members of the public. Checklist 10.6 gives some examples.

Checklist 10.6   **Examples of preventive measures to combat violence to staff**

- Change the job to reduce face-to-face contact (e.g. use automatic ticket machines, cash dispensers).
- Move from cash to cheque, credit cards, vouchers, tokens.
- Make sure staff can get home safely.
- Train staff to spot aggression early and deal with it.
- Change the layout of public waiting areas to reduce the tension of waiting.
- Use wider counters etc.
- Install cctv/video cameras and alarm buttons.
- Put protective screens around staff areas.
- Use coded security locks on doors to keep public out of staff areas.

Step 5: involve staff in designing safety measures.

Step 6: put measures into practice.

Step 7: check that the implemented measures work.

Discrimination

Research published in 1995 showed that after 20 years of equality legislation, certain workplaces were more prone to discriminatory practices than others (Milward, 1995). This research, published by the Equal Opportunities Commission, looked at the composition of different workforces by gender and found that:

- in the manufacturing sector, only the clothing industry employed a majority of women
- women's jobs predominated in the service industries, retailing, education and medical services
- the majority of clerical and administrative workers were women
- the majority of skilled workers, senior professional, technical and managerial staff were men

(to which, as a woman, my response is 'Tell me something new!') The researchers concluded that where job segregation occurred, discrimination was more likely to be prevalent. Women employees working with other women were likely to be paid less than male employees working with other men.

The various Acts designed to promote equal opportunities in the workplace, such as the Sex Discrimination Acts 1975 and 1986, the Race Relations Act 1976, the Disability Discrimination Act 1995 and the Equal Pay Act 1970 (amended 1983) have all sought to reduce discriminatory practices. Checklist 10.7 details the areas in which discrimination – not only against women but against people of non-British race and people with disabilities – commonly occur. You might like to consider whether discriminatory practices occur in your own organisation in any of these areas.

Checklist 10.7 **Areas where discrimination may operate**

- recruitment
- selection
- training and development
- pay
- promotion
- pregnancy
- the operation of grievance disputes and disciplinary procedures
- retirement
- dismissal
- redundancy

In many cases, it is illegal in the European Union to discriminate against any category of employee in relation to recruitment and selection, pay for work of equal worth, promotion, pregnancy, retirement, dismissal or redundancy, but the bringing of a case depends on the knowledge and ability of the individual being discriminated against. Look at the two examples below where discrimination in selection was proved in both cases.

Example 12

Elke was a well qualified candidate for the job but was turned down by her Dutch employers because she was pregnant at the time of her application. Under the Dutch social insurance scheme, an employer would have to pay her and her replacement while she was on maternity leave. Despite the fact that the employer would have had to pay two salaries during the period of statutory maternity leave, their refusal to employ her was held to be discriminatory (*Personnel Manager's Factbook*).

Example 13

The Asian Cultural Centre had advertised for an assistant director and Zia thought she had a good chance of getting the job since she met all the selection critiera. However, she was not shortlisted. When she rang the Centre to enquire why she had failed to get past this first hurdle, she was told she did not meet the requirements of other criteria that had been established after all the applications had been received. Zia took the case to an industrial tribunal, which found that not only did the Centre not employ any Asian staff, but none of the applicants of Asian origin had been shortlisted. They ruled in Zia's favour that the Centre was guilty of unlawful discrimination.

Like harassment, bullying and violence, discrimination by one employee against another on the basis of gender, race, religion or disability should be treated as a disciplinary offence and this should be stated in the written rules and procedures. Sometimes discrimination is operated through ignorance and by accident. For example, if you look at the composition of the workforce in your organisation, can you see any evidence that:

- fewer individuals from under-represented groups such as women or ethnic minorities apply for employment or promotion?
- fewer individuals than would be expected from these groups are recruited or promoted?
- these groups are under-represented in training or in senior jobs in the organisation?
- these groups are concentrated in certain shifts or in sections or departments?

If any of the above are the case, then you should consider whether overt discrimination is taking place. If it is, not only is there a danger that a case will be brought against the organisation by an employee at some point, but your organisation may already be contravening the law.

Redundancy

Although there is a wealth of advice and legislation surrounding the practice of redundancy, too many organisations will handle this very emotive event in an insensitive way. I have heard at first hand of people receiving their notice of redundancy in their pay packet with no prior warning; of more senior staff being called in to their manager's office and being told they are to be made redundant with effect from the end of that week. In most cases, such behaviour is inexcusable, however much the organisation may be under pressure.

People who are to be made redundant have certain rights, and these are outlined in Checklist 10.8.

Checklist 10.8 Rights of redundant employees

Every employee who is made redundant has the right to:

- paid time off work to look for another job
- paid time off work to arrange training
- redundancy pay
- notice
- a trial period in alternative work in the organisation without jeopardising the right to their entitlement to redundancy pay

There are also a number of factors that affect the degree to which dismissal for redundancy is normally accepted to be fair. These are outlined in Checklist 10.9 and discussed in more detail below.

Checklist 10.9 Redundancy as a fair reason for dismissal

Dismissal for redundancy will normally be fair as long as:

- the redundancy is genuine
- redundant personnel have been chosen on the basis of agreed criteria
- elected employee representatives have been consulted
- there is no suitable work available
- selection for redundancy does not contravene any of the Acts governing discriminatory practices

Redundancy must be seen to be genuine and not an excuse to get rid of lazy, underperforming or incapable employees. Normally, it is the job that is made redundant, not the jobholder. So if a person is made redundant and the job continues, being taken on by another jobholder, the redundant employee may successfully claim for unfair dismissal.

It doesn't matter what the criteria for making employees redundant are, but they do need to have been agreed and published beforehand. Interestingly, this is an area where it may be possible to get rid of staff who are underperforming. For example, the organisation may make persistent absenteeism, or failure to meet targets, part of the criteria for redundancy.

Employers have the choice of consultation with recognised, independent trade unions or with elected employee representatives over the manner and methods of making staff redundant.

An employer is not bound to find, or create, alternative work opportunities for its redundant employees but it is expected to notify employees of alternative job opportunities if these exist. The employees usually need to apply in the normal way and are subject to the same selection criteria as anyone else.

Employers that contravene any of the Acts governing discriminatory practices when making staff redundant face the likelihood of having to pay compensation. One of the problem areas here is that of part-time workers. Often, employers may want to make part-time workers redundant before full-time workers. But since the majority of part-time workers are women, this could be seen as a discriminatory practice (*Personnel Manager's Factbook*).

➡ HANDLING THE SITUATION

So far you have been looking at a number of examples of sensitive situations in the workplace and at the regulatory and legal minefields that surround them. In this final section, you are going to be considering how you, as a manager, can handle these situations sensitively and thoughtfully, reconciling the interests of your employers and the staff for whom you are responsible.

Below are a number of short scenarios that first-year MBA students are asked to consider in their management of people. Read through each one and think about how you might handle an interview with the other person.

Example 14

A member of your staff arrives half an hour late for work. This is the fifth time this has happened. The excuse is that they had to take their child to the childminder because their partner was unable to do so.

Example 15

One of your staff returns from an extended lunch break, unsteady on her feet and reeking of drink.

Example 16

Overtime is absolutely essential if your department is going to meet its target. You have no other staff member available and the one you approach refuses because he has to pick up his child from the nursery.

Example 17

An employee comes into your office and complains that, yet again, the temperature in the building at the start of the day's work is unacceptably low. There have been frequent complaints before from members of your staff and you have contacted Office Services but nothing has been done.

Example 18

An employee comes in and says she doesn't like to 'grass' on a workmate but she has just seen a colleague secreting company property into his private bag.

Example 19

You receive a complaint from an employee that the staff in one of your units have displayed a calendar with pornographic pictures that he finds offensive. Although only men work in that unit, women customers often visit it.

Example 20

You notice that one of your staff has a number of bruises on her face and arms. On asking her how these occurred, she says she was attacked by one of the packers when she went to the cloakroom but didn't like to make an issue of it.

And I could go on. Workplaces might appear to be hotbeds of problems, difficult and perverted people, violence and harassment. While we all know they are not really like this, sometimes situations do occur – usually when we are least prepared – that need to be dealt with very quickly if not immediately.

Much of what you read in Chapter 2 on communication is important in the context of coping with sensitive situations at work, particularly the skill of actively listening to the other person. When someone comes to you with an alleged grievance or complaint, you need to make time to listen to what they say and gather as much information – *factual* information – as you can from the individual. This needs, as we saw earlier, to be recorded in writing and supported by evidence from other people involved in, or observing, the incident.

Already, in Examples 14–20 above, you would have been employing three communication skills: active listening, interviewing to elicit information, and keeping an accurate written record. You should add to these the skill of adopting a counselling approach towards those who are upset or angry about alleged grievances and the need for complete objectivity in a disciplinary situation.

Adopting a counselling approach is not the same as 'counselling'. The latter is a very skilled technique, requiring formal training and should not be attempted by an amateur. Indeed, one of the decisions you may need to make from time to time as a manager is at what point you need to bring in specialist help. For example, an employee who is obviously suffering from excessive stress or is showing signs of depression almost certainly needs medical help. Someone who is particularly upset at the treatment they have received, such as harassment, violence or bullying, may well need to see a trained counsellor to help them work through the experience. Checklist 10.10 outlines some of the different ways in which a manager can take a counselling approach to a member of staff in a sensitive situation.

Checklist 10.10 **Elements of a counselling approach**

- identifying key issues and asking the employee to reflect on these
- asking the employee to make an analysis of the situation and why it might have arisen
- empathising with the employee ('I know what you mean/how you feel.')
- asking for clarification ('Is that what you mean?')
- encouraging the employee to talk openly
- being non-judgmental
- remaining calm and patient regardless of the emotional state of the employee
- checking out assumptions made on the basis of incomplete information
- probing for further information

The best solution to the situation is often the one that the employee comes up with and feels he or she 'owns'. People may listen to advice, but they may not take it and it may not be appropriate.

In many situations you will have your part of a bargain to keep. Look back at the quotation with which I started this chapter. If you agree to take some specific action to alleviate a sensitive situation, then you need to ensure that you actually do it. But you should avoid making assumptions. Look at the two examples below – they are the same example but the manager acted differently in each case.

Example 21a

Ann asked to see her manager to make a formal complaint about the continued sexual harassment she alleged she was undergoing. She told her manager that her supervisor was always making suggestive remarks to her and putting pressure on her to go out with him. The manager was furious since the company prided itself on its equal opportunities policy and any sexist or racist behaviour was treated very seriously. He told Ann that the supervisor would be disciplined and moved to another department.

Example 21b

In the same case, the manager listened to what Ann had to say, checking on facts such as when the incidents had occurred and how long they had been going on. He promised to speak to one or two of the other women in the department before deciding what further action to take. In the meantime, he suggested Ann take a week's paid leave of absence.

In the first case, the manager was assuming guilt on the part of the supervisor without checking on any facts. Had he or she followed through the promised action, the supervisor might have brought a counter-complaint if he believed he was being victimised. In the second case, the manager was being more cautious. This didn't mean he was treating the case any less seriously but he felt he couldn't take one person's word for it. This was the right course of action to suggest. Cases like this can be very much more complex than they appear at first. For example, under investigation, the second manager could have found out that Ann and the supervisor had been having an affair for several months but it had recently come to an end at the supervisor's instigation.

➡ **CHRIS'S PROBLEM (10)**

You are conscious that there seems to be a higher-than-average number of problems occurring in Chris's department. Not only have there been three formal grievances brought in the last six months but now you have been asked to take part in what looks like a very serious case of discipline. On asking Chris for records of the individual's behaviour, Chris replies 'What records? Everyone knows he is a pain in the neck – you only need to talk to his workmates and you'll see what I mean. I've told him again and again that I won't stand for it any more until I really lost my temper with him and he hit me. That was the last straw and I told him he was in for the high jump which was when I called you in. What more evidence do you need than my black eye?'

What advice would you offer Chris on dealing with sensitive situations?

References

Milward R., *Targeting Potential Discrimination* (Equal Opportunities Commission, London, 1995)

Owen K., *A Legal Framework for Managers* (The Open University Press, Milton Keynes, 1995)

Personnel Manager's Factbook (Gee, 1997)

Ray J., *English Proverbs* (1670)

Sexual Harassment in the Workplace (HMSO, Norwich, date)

Violence at Work (Health and Safety Executive, London, 1996)

Index